FROM THE BIBLE-TEACHING MINISTRY OF

CHARLES R. SWINDOLL

Exquisitely Imperfect

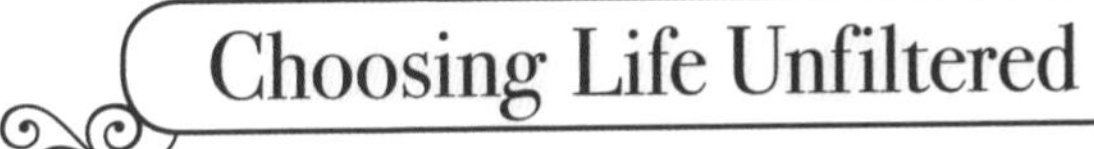
Choosing Life Unfiltered

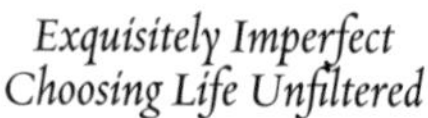

Exquisitely Imperfect
Choosing Life Unfiltered

From the Bible-Teaching Ministry of Charles R. Swindoll

Charles R. Swindoll has devoted his life to the accurate, practical teaching and application of God's Word and His grace. A pastor at heart, Chuck has served as senior pastor to congregations in Massachusetts, California, and Texas. Since 1998, he has served as the founder and senior pastor-teacher of Stonebriar Community Church in Frisco, Texas, but Chuck's listening audience extends far beyond a local church body. As a leading program in Christian broadcasting since 1979, *Insight for Living* airs in major Christian radio markets around the world, reaching people groups in languages they can understand. Chuck's extensive writing ministry has also served the body of Christ worldwide, and his leadership as president and now chancellor of Dallas Theological Seminary has helped prepare and equip a new generation of men and women for ministry. Chuck and Cynthia, his partner in life and ministry, have four grown children, ten grandchildren, and six great-grandchildren.

Published By:
IFL Publishing House
A Division of Insight for Living Ministries
Post Office Box 5000, Frisco, Texas 75034-0055

EDITOR IN CHIEF: Cynthia Swindoll, President, Insight for Living Ministries
EXECUTIVE VICE PRESIDENT: Wayne Stiles, Th.M., D.Min., Dallas Theological Seminary
SENIOR VICE PRESIDENT: Mark T. Tobey, Th.M., Dallas Theological Seminary
WRITERS:
Joni Halpin, B.S., Accountancy, Miami University
Malia Rodriguez, Th.M., Dallas Theological Seminary
Robyn Roste, Bachelor of Journalism, Thompson Rivers University
Sharifa Stevens, Th.M., Dallas Theological Seminary
LeeAnna Swartz, B.A., Communications, Moody Bible Institute
SUBSTANTIVE EDITOR: Jim Craft, M.A., English, Mississippi College; Certificate of Biblical and Theological Studies, Dallas Theological Seminary
COPY EDITOR: Paula McCoy, B.A., English, Texas A&M University-Commerce
PROJECT SUPERVISOR, CREATIVE MINISTRIES: Megan Meckstroth, B.S., Advertising, University of Florida; Certificate in Project Management, Southern Methodist University
PROJECT MANAGER, PUBLISHING: Rachael Deatherage, Communications Project Manager, Insight for Living Ministries
ASSISTANT TO THE EVP/CCO: Abby McClure, B.S., Marketing, Dallas Baptist University
PROOFREADER: LeeAnna Swartz, B.A., Communications, Moody Bible Institute
DESIGNER: Laura Dubroc, B.F.A., Advertising Design, University of Louisiana at Lafayette
PRODUCTION ARTIST: Nancy Gustine, B.F.A., Advertising Art, University of North Texas

ISBN: (Paperback edition) 978-1-62655-123-7
ISBN: (e-book edition) 978-1-62655-124-4
Printed in the United States of America

Table of Contents

About the Writers

Joni Halpin

B.S., Accountancy, Miami University

Joni received an accounting degree from Miami University in Oxford, Ohio. After eight years on staff with Campus Crusade for Christ (Cru), Joni worked in healthcare finance while earning her CPA license. The discovery of her passion for writing and editing led Joni to a new career. She now serves at Insight for Living Ministries in the Web Ministries Department, where she writes and edits content, manages the ministry's social media accounts, and oversees Chuck Swindoll's daily devotionals. Joni and her husband live in the Dallas area, where she has served at her church as a writer and editor for more than fifteen years.

Malia Rodriguez

Th.M., Dallas Theological Seminary

Malia received her master of theology degree in Systematic Theology from Dallas Theological Seminary. She now serves as a writer in the Creative Ministries Department of Insight for Living Ministries, where she is able to merge her love of theology with her gift for words. Malia and her husband, Matt, who is also a graduate of Dallas Theological Seminary, live in the Dallas area with their son and daughter.

Robyn Roste
Bachelor of Journalism, Thompson Rivers University

As manager of media and marketing at Insight for Living Canada, Robyn serves the ministry as a writer, editor, and broadcast producer. She works in Abbotsford, B.C., where she also lives on a rural acreage with her husband. Robyn enjoys blogging, jogging, and knitting and plays slo-pitch in her spare time.

Sharifa Stevens
Th.M., Dallas Theological Seminary

A New York native, Sharifa earned a bachelor of arts degree from Columbia University before moving to Dallas, Texas, where she received a master of theology degree from Dallas Theological Seminary. She currently serves as a writer for the Creative Ministries Department of Insight for Living Ministries. Sharifa is passionate about worship through music and the intersection of faith and culture. She is wife to a Renaissance man and mother to two lively boys.

LeeAnna Swartz
B.A., Communications, Moody Bible Institute

A native of Texas, LeeAnna met her husband, Ethan, while they both attended Moody Bible Institute in Chicago. After graduating from Moody, LeeAnna and Ethan moved to the Dallas area where Ethan attended Dallas Theological Seminary, graduating in December 2016. LeeAnna currently serves at Insight for Living Ministries as a proofreader, editor, and contributing writer. LeeAnna recently gave birth to their first child.

A Note from Someone like You

by

Colleen Swindoll Thompson

Dear Beautiful Woman:

I know you've felt it. I sure have. We *all* have — the pressure to be something that doesn't exist: the perfect woman. As I sat down at my computer to write you, just for kicks I searched these exact words, *How to be the perfect woman.* Within a millisecond, almost 15,000,000 sites, videos, and other links lit up my screen.

I clicked on one. It turned out to be a page written by a man who asserted that the "perfect woman" changes with age. Now isn't that helpful? I immediately thought of molting hermit crabs, the process they go through when shedding a shell they have outgrown. As they get ready to change shells, hermit crabs give off "molting signs," affectionately called the "Pre-Molting Stages" or PMS, scout's honor! They get all crabby, wanting to be left alone as they move from their small shell into bigger, better digs.

Next, I checked out an exhausting six-part, multipage outline that had so many definitions and to-do lists, it could make bank if it were a smartphone app! One of the other sites that popped up in my search combined thirteen different celebrity facial features to make the "perfect" face. The only thing missing was a scratch and sniff sticker near the neck, revealing the perfume of choice! If I spent a fortune at the Mall of America and a lifetime at a plastic surgeon's office, I still wouldn't look like the glamorous concoction this site so flagrantly deemed "perfect." No one would.

Sadly, in all my reading, I found very little difference between Christian opinions and secular ones. From *Cosmopolitan* and *Men's Health* to a few Christian magazines (I won't name) — the search was disheartening and empty, unapologetically brash and excessively conflicted.

Everywhere we look, there's someone telling us how to walk the line. You've got to work more or stay at home more. Get fit or live a little. Keep your skin young or embrace your age. Fear one thing; control another. You're a failure if you don't feed your kids the perfect, healthy (and delicious!) homemade foods. You're less of a woman if you can't make all your husband's dreams come true. You're a disgrace if you draw the wrong kind of attention; you're not enough if you can't hold on to the right kind.

No wonder we struggle as women to find our identity!

Too often, we get lost in the pursuit to please others and have it (and be it) all. *New York Times* best-selling author David Brooks, in *The Road to Character*, sums up our faulty human thinking about success:

> When we think about making a difference or leading a life with purpose, we often think of achieving something external — performing some service that will have an impact on the world, creating a successful company, or doing something for the community.[1]

Continuing that thought, Richard Rohr writes in *Falling Upward*:

> The very unfortunate result of this preoccupation with order, control, safety, pleasure, and certitude is that a high percentage of people never get to the contents of their own lives! . . . Much of organized religion, however, tends to be peopled by folks who have a mania for some ideal order, which is never true, so they are seldom happy or content. . . . "If you are not perfect, then *you* are doing something wrong."[2]

Beautiful woman, are you tired of feeling confused, conflicted, unworthy, and unfulfilled? Have you fallen into depression from measuring your value by how much money you make, how many degrees you've earned, or worse, if your house looks like a Pinterest page and your Facebook pictures have so many likes?

PLEASE!

Tune out the countless blogs, videos, magazines, books, social media sites, men, and other women who tell you what you need to do or be or change to measure up! Tune out your own voice if you have to. There's only one voice — *one single voice* — that defines you: the voice of the One who made you.

God created *every* part of you. He knows you. He loves you. And He promises to never leave you. Remember what He told us in the very first book of His Word? "In the image of God he created them; male and female he created them" (Genesis 1:27). You, yes, YOU are part of God's crowning creative work — made in His image. Who you are, your existence and your essence, is defined by God and God alone.

Growing up, I must've heard my dad tell me this statement every week:

Colleen, in life, you must . . .

1. *Know who you are*
2. *Like who you are*
3. *Be who you are*

Throughout my life, I have struggled deeply with depression, fear, mindfulness, self-worth, and shattered dreams. I have felt insignificant, unable to balance life's responsibilities and answer my questions about faith. It's my guess that these may be some of the very battles you're facing today. I've learned these are symptoms of a deeper conflict — an uncertain, unstable identity. So won't you join me and some of my favorite women as we examine the areas where we struggle and come to terms with who God made each of us to be?

Before you turn the page, let me ask you: Beautiful woman, do you know who you are? Do you like who you are? Are you able to be who you are?

If you're looking for another way to try to be perfect, this book won't help. But if you're ready to feel comfortable in your own skin, confident in who you are and who God desires you to be, you've come to the right place. This book is all about helping you become YOU . . . exactly who God made you to be . . . someone you can know and like and be free to be.

With love and hope,

Colleen Swindoll Thompson

Endnotes

1. David Brooks, *The Road to Character* (New York: Random House, 2015), 9.
2. Richard Rohr, *Falling Upward: A Spirituality for the Two Halves of Life* (San Francisco: Jossey-Bass, 2011), 7, 60 – 61.

Exquisitely Imperfect

Choosing Life Unfiltered

Confessions of a People-Pleaser

Obviously, I'm not trying to win the approval of people, but of God. If pleasing people were my goal, I would not be Christ's servant.

~Galatians 1:10

"He that respects himself is safe from others; he wears a coat of mail that none can pierce."
—Henry Wadsworth Longfellow[1]

I'd had a great day at work. I had received unexpected praise from my boss and a coworker, leaving me with renewed confidence. I'd had an invigorating discussion with a good friend at lunch — the kind where we were both able to speak into each other's lives and encourage each other's walk with God. As I drove home, the cloud formations were unusually colorful and scenic. To top it off, one of my favorite "feel-good" songs came up on my playlist — and it finished right as I rolled into the garage.

My husband, Joe, a computer programmer, worked at home at that time. As I bounced into his office, I heard his frustrated sigh.

"Hi, Hubby. How's your day been?"

"Don't even ask. First, I lost about three hours of work. Since then, I haven't been able to get my code to work right, and I have no idea why. I've made zero progress today. It's driving me crazy!"

Immediately, I went into damage control mode. Without even knowing I was doing it, I jettisoned right out the window all my positive feelings and took on Joe's negative ones. Rather than telling him how well *my* day went, I tried to be a sensitive, sympathetic wife by keeping it all to myself.

Later that evening, a good friend called to see if I wanted to go to a movie with her on Saturday afternoon. I had just read a review of that movie and decided it was one I preferred to pass up. Besides, I was really looking forward to getting caught up on laundry and a few other chores. But that sounded like a lame excuse, and I thought about how disappointed she might be if I turned her down, so I said I'd love to join her.

Do you sense something wrong in the narratives above? At the time, I thought I was simply being a good wife and a good friend. Years later, I can now tell you I had a serious boundary problem!

"Boundaries" get talked about often as something we need to be healthy. But what exactly are boundaries? And why are they important to have? Learning the answers to those questions has been at least a fifteen-year journey for me, and the learning continues daily. In their classic book *Boundaries*, Drs. Henry Cloud and John Townsend explained: "Boundaries define us. They define *what is me* and *what is not me*. A boundary shows me where I end and someone else begins, leading me to a sense of ownership."[2] Effective boundaries encompass the physical, the emotional, the mental, *and* the spiritual.

Imagine if you went out to mow your lawn, but no one had ever told you where your lawn ends and your neighbor's begins. Could you finish the task? Similar confusion and frustration result in our lives when we have no boundaries to define ourselves. It makes it impossible for us to nurture and maintain our minds, bodies, and souls. Humans need boundaries, because we function within relationships. If we all lived alone and had no contact with anyone else, we wouldn't have to worry about healthy boundaries. But relationships are inherent to the human experience.

I'm a self-confessed conflict-avoider, otherwise known as a people-pleaser. Here's how my thoughts often break down:

I want others to approve of what I do and say, and I want to keep peace between us at all costs. Because of this, I allow myself to take on responsibility for what *they* feel, how *they* react to what I say, and even for how *they* treat me. Multiple problems result from this kind of thinking.

First, no one has to take responsibility for their own feelings and actions when they're around me. They're off the hook. I'll take on the burden, and I certainly won't let anyone know when a word spoken or an action taken hurts me. So chances are, the people I interact with won't be able to grow and refine their own behavior when we're together. I've prevented any iron from sharpening iron (Proverbs 27:17). Galatians 6:7–8 reminds us that whatever we sow, we will also reap. My faulty thinking inhibits others from reaping what they've sown, at least for a time, and it causes me to sow seeds I never intended.

Second, if I'm busy taking on other people's feelings, how am I ever going to discover who *I* really am? If I never allow myself to feel and express my true feelings, those feelings get repressed and unidentified. Without knowing why, I become increasingly irritable, unfulfilled, and over time, depressed.

Does that sound like a woman who's comfortable in her own skin and ready to embrace who God desires her to be? Hardly.

At the risk of oversimplifying, most people fall into one of two categories: people-pleasers who have no boundaries or boundary-busters who cross boundaries. Boundary-busters might be controlling, domineering individuals who take advantage of people-pleasers. But they can just as easily simply be oblivious to how their actions and words affect others.

I don't have to spell out the toxic effects of a people-pleaser and a boundary-buster living together without any insight into their tendencies nor skills to identify and lovingly enforce healthy boundaries.

I've observed that most people aren't even aware of the concept of healthy boundaries, just as I wasn't for far too long. Countless relational problems could be resolved if we could just learn where our responsibilities end and others' begin. When two people in a relationship both clearly state their boundaries and agree to try their best to respect the other's, they create a safe, loving atmosphere of mutual respect where each person can thrive. Don't we all long for that?

My ongoing challenge in asserting healthy boundaries is expressing them in love, not with a firm or angry, No! Sadly, some situations do call for that degree of firmness. But most of the time, if I gently state my desires or expectations, the other person understands and adjusts accordingly. Those who care about me really want to know my boundaries. When I express them openly, I deliver the people I interact with from all kinds of second-guessing and mind reading. Plus, I've no "need" to practice passive-aggressive behavior (a favorite tactic for us people-pleasers!).

A Wall or a Boundary?

When I first started learning about boundaries, I thought they seemed a bit harsh, even selfish. But then, with the help of wise mentors and friends, I learned the difference between boundaries and walls. Walls are rigid and unmovable. Boundaries are not. The boundaries I put in place for one person may not be necessary for another. And as I see a particular relationship grow in a healthy way, I may be able to remove some of my boundaries.

My boundaries aren't necessarily the same as yours. Each of us has a unique set of experiences, inclinations, and needs that dictate what boundaries we should have in our individual relationships. For example, a woman with an abusive past will need stronger boundaries than mine, at least while healing takes place. And a woman with a history of taking advantage of other people will need a whole different set of boundaries. One woman may be able to learn to practice healthy boundaries with the help of a close friend; another may need to talk it out with a good counselor.

Here's the wonderful part—no one's responsible for defining and enforcing your boundaries but *you*. That's because no one but you knows your heart and your motives. After you have identified your boundaries and learned how to enforce them, you'll gain the insight to know when to stand firm and when to bend. You'll be making intentional decisions that will empower you and the people you care about.

So, in other words, if I want to bust my own boundary as an appropriate act of love and sacrifice, I can. How freeing!

For example, let's say I had been strong enough to tell my friend no to going to that movie and been able to do it in a healthy way. What would that mean? First of all, it would mean that I had learned I wasn't responsible for her reaction to my turning down her request. Second, it would mean that I had recognized my voice and allowed myself to choose to say no and to tell her the reason for my no . . . or not. No explanation would have been required. Third, it would mean that I had learned that my desire to catch up on laundry and chores is just as valid as her desire to see a movie.

Now let's say that after I'd said no, in the middle of doing my chores, I received a call from my friend in the lobby of the theater. Through tears, she tells me she just found out her mother passed away. Of course, I would drop everything to be by her side. But doing so would be *my* choice. And it would align with my desire to be Christlike. After all, Jesus allowed His schedule to be disrupted by pleas to come and help. He willingly went out of His way because of His heart of compassion.

I once heard someone explain having healthy, moveable boundaries with the phrase "for fun and for free." She said one way to test if your boundary is being inappropriately busted is to ask yourself, *Can I do this for fun and for free?* Can I say yes out of a full willingness to serve and no fear of rejection, without bitterness or regret, and with no strings attached? If I can, I should go for it (2 Corinthians 9:7). If not, I must trust that God can find someone else to fill the need while I tackle higher priorities.

Again, boundaries are not walls. Our to-do list changes. The amount of sleep we get changes. The degree of emotional expenditure that's required of us changes. Our ratio of fun to work changes. We all need to practice *balance*, as we determine, enforce, and flex our boundaries. (Balance could be the subject of a whole book on its own!)

Free to Disagree?

How could I have reacted in a more healthy way to my husband's frustrating day? Of course, it was appropriate to show Joe sympathy and understanding and to validate his feelings. But because my feelings were equally as valid, I could have also told him, without apology, how *my* day went. After expressing my support, I could have said, "I wish your day had gone the way mine did. Let me tell you about it."

Who knows — my good news and attitude might have lightened his mood! Maybe that was even one reason God gave me such a good experience that day. Maybe, if I had refused to take on Joe's emotions, he would have more quickly been able to get past them and put them in a healthier, long-term perspective. I'll never know, because I chose to jump down into the pit with Joe instead of extending him a hand to help pull him out.

God has lovingly shown me that I often suppress my emotions out of fear. That day with Joe, I thought, *What if he gets angry and calls me insensitive for daring to be upbeat?* Looking back, I doubt my husband would have reacted that way, but even if he had, it would have been *his* responsibility, not mine (Ephesians 4:26). I've learned, ever so slowly, that I have to allow Joe the dignity of living his own life and experiencing the consequences of his behavior. That isn't likely to happen as long as I let fear govern my actions. Fear keeps us from being ourselves and celebrating the differences in others.

Have you ever been around a person who simply echoes everything you say and never asserts an additional thought or contrary opinion? Didn't spending time with that person get boring? Sooner or later, you run out of things to talk about, and you realize you could've had the same conversation if you'd just been talking to the mirror. (I've wondered if Joe used to feel that way about me, but I'm not about to ask him!)

I Gotta Be Me!

I'm extremely grateful that God has patiently taught me that He made me unique for a reason. To be a good steward of the unique life, talents, and gifts He has given me, I *first* have to be free to discover them. Having boundaries is an active way of living — of taking charge instead of waiting for things to happen to me or for others to direct me.

Over time, I've learned that only when I'm free to say no to another's ideas of how I should invest my life am I fully available for God to develop my uniqueness and shape me into the beautiful woman *He* wants me to be. My reflection of the image of God looks different from yours, and we can marvel in that difference and give God the glory.

As you learn to embrace who you are and who others are by establishing and maintaining healthy boundaries, remember that "no one can know a person's thoughts except that person's own spirit, and no one can know God's thoughts except God's own Spirit" (1 Corinthians 2:11). We usually won't know why other people define their boundaries the way they do. And we needn't know. That's between God and them (Matthew 7:1–2).

As we soak in God's Word and learn to base our identities in who He says we are, we can relax and live in peace with our boundaries, regardless of how others react to them. Then, and only then, will we be ready for the grand adventures of freedom God has designed our lives to be (2 Corinthians 3:17; Galatians 5:1).

Could You Have Said (or Done) This?

In light of what you have just read about boundaries, read each of the following verses and ask yourself:

How did Jesus demonstrate a healthy boundary in this situation? Could you have reacted in the same way He did? Why, or why not?

1. Matthew 19:21–22: Jesus' reply to the rich young ruler
2. Matthew 14:22–23: When Jesus drew apart for time alone
3. Luke 6:9–11: Jesus' choice to heal on the Sabbath
4. Matthew 16:21–23: Jesus' rebuke of Peter
5. Luke 23:8–10: Jesus in front of Herod

—Joni Halpin

Endnotes

1. Henry Wadsworth Longfellow, in *Courage to Change: One Day at a Time in Al-Anon II*, (Virginia Beach, Va., Al-Anon, 1992), 345.
2. Henry Cloud and John Townsend, *Boundaries* (Grand Rapids: Zondervan, 1992), 31.

I'll Do It Later

Don't put it off; do it now!
Don't rest until you do.

~ Proverbs 6:4

"I've spent *how much* on credit card interest and late fees in the past three months?"

The customer service representative replied, "You don't want to know. In fact, you don't want to know how much you've spent in the past three years on interest and late fees."

"But I pay my credit card off every month! How can I have so many fees?"

"You pay it off, yes. But you don't pay on time. The penalty for late payments is a late fee plus interest charges on every purchase for the next two months. If you pay late the next month, the penalty starts over."

"But I didn't know . . ." With tears spilling down my face, I let my sentence trail off, lest my voice betray my emotion. Before making the call contesting my latest bill I resolved not to cry. *Must remain stoic.*

"We aren't responsible for your lack of knowledge. This information was all in the terms you received when you signed up for this card."

Biting back an angry reply, I took a deep breath and closed my eyes. This conversation was not going my way. How was I supposed to know about penalties hidden in the fine print? No one reads the fine print! I shouldn't be required to memorize it! And why do they charge so many fees and such high interest? I only ever paid my bills a couple days late. A week late at most. They should look at my bill payment history and know I'm good for it . . . eventually. However, deep down, I knew I wouldn't get the fees and interest removed. Even though I didn't understand the rules of using a credit card, I had broken them and had to pay the price.

I was humiliated, frustrated, and terrified. And because I lacked understanding, I avoided my bills altogether. This meant late payments, lost checks, and piles of unopened mail on the counter.

As the financial impact of my inaction sunk in, I wondered how avoiding financial responsibility might be viewed by God—as well as by others in the body of Christ. While the Bible doesn't say "Thou shalt not procrastinate," I knew avoiding responsibility wasn't a godly biblical concept. Colossians 3:23 says everything I do should be done for the Lord. *Procrastination*, to paraphrase the dictionary, is a willful delay of doing something that should be done. If I'm willfully delaying paying my bills, then it's as if I'm also doing this unto the Lord. So it's wrong.

I knew it was time to make a change and get my head out of the sand, but I didn't know how to begin changing my bad habits. After reflection, I realized my behavior was rooted in fear, which was not from the Lord (2 Timothy 1:7). It was time to stop procrastinating.

As I thought about how to accomplish this change, I considered all the reasons I should keep doing things the way I had done. Sure, it was unorganized chaos, but it was familiar and comfortable. I knew what to expect. It was easy to keep things the same. Instead, I decided to change—which was hard, awkward, and painful. I listed my excuses for procrastinating and then dealt with them one by one.

I don't know where to start.

In my mind, money was a big, green bully, and I was the little bug it cruelly squished. I needed help learning to manage my finances—and James 1:5 told me where to look. "If you need wisdom, ask our generous God, and he will give it to you. He will not rebuke you for asking." Time to pray.

I can't understand money.

Maybe, I had avoided asking God for help because I felt ashamed for not understanding it. But it was the truth, and the only way to begin to change was by admitting I didn't have a clue how to handle money. In my searching for biblical wisdom, Proverbs 2:2, 6 gave me more encouragement.

> *Tune your ears to wisdom,*
> *and concentrate on understanding. . . .*
> *For the* Lord *grants wisdom!*
> *From his mouth come knowledge and understanding.*

With some anxiety, I asked God for wisdom and understanding. The next Sunday at church, my pastor told the congregation about a free six-week budgeting course for anyone who wanted to learn how to make and balance a budget. So I signed up.

I'm overwhelmed with the amount I have to learn.

The man leading the budgeting course spent most of the first evening explaining what to expect and the emotional reactions we may experience as a result of the coursework. He told us it's normal to feel overwhelmed. I looked around the room and noticed people of all ages. People older than I didn't know how to budget either? Were they afraid too? Knowing I wasn't alone in my ignorance helped me accept feeling overwhelmed and begin moving past my fear.

I'm afraid I won't have enough money to achieve my goals.

We were challenged to tailor our budgets according to the financial goals we wanted to accomplish. I didn't know a budgeter could do that. Up until then, I thought a budget was an immutable, standardized document that a person was required to live up to. I had never thought about my financial goals before—objectives I wanted to achieve and how much I needed in order to accomplish them.

In an instant, budgeting became a way I could plan and set financial goals in order to do more things in life that I wanted to do. Instead of being the bully who squished me, money transformed into a pal who could help me reach my goals.

What if it's too much hard work?

My first budget took me more than a week to balance. Receipts littered my kitchen table, and my recycling bin overflowed with mistake-riddled budget templates. Proverbs 12:24 says, "Work hard and become a leader; / be lazy and become a slave." Dealing with money was hard work, but I was beginning to see where the proper money management could take me.

The more I learned about money, the more I saw how enslaved I'd been by my lack of financial knowledge. Putting in the hours to gain insight not only transformed my grasp on financial concepts but it empowered me to take responsibility for my money.

What if I'm bad at managing my money?

After completing my budgeting course, I confronted a new fear. I had a balanced budget. I had financial goals. I had put in the work. But what if I failed?

Proverbs 16:3 gave me courage: "Commit your actions to the LORD, / and your plans will succeed."

Overcoming financial procrastination began as a desire to be a better testament to God. I wanted to honor Him with my finances, so I put in the work in order to stop avoiding what was right. I began trusting that He would continue leading me down the path of financial independence.

I wish I could say my relationship with money was the only place procrastination popped up. Turns out, I love putting things off until tomorrow. Writing deadlines, homework, grocery shopping, getting out of bed, getting dressed for work, exercising . . . I could go on. In the moment, procrastination feels amazing, but it only leads to anxiety.

Whenever I need motivation, I look at how The Message renders Ecclesiastes 9:10.

> *Each day is God's gift. It's all you get in exchange*
> *For the hard work of staying alive.*
> *Make the most of each one!*
> *Whatever turns up, grab it and do it. And heartily!*
> *This is your last and only chance at it,*
> *For there's neither work to do nor thoughts to think*
> *In the company of the dead, where you're most certainly headed.*

I love this—*Whatever turns up, grab it and do it. And heartily!*

As I meditate on God's Word, I can look forward to making the most of each day. Solomon was right; we're not here for long, so let's take up his challenge to make the most of our days and leave procrastination for later.

Procrastination: Living Costly

One of the biggest challenges young adults face is transitioning to financial independence.

I sure miss the safety and security of the days when my parents paid for me to live, and my babysitting money put gas in my car and fast food in my stomach.

But, of course, the responsibility of paying to live is only the beginning of financial independence. Once we make the transition from dependence to self-reliance, new challenges arise.

For example, which brand of fruit should we buy? The imported fruit from the big store is cheaper and more convenient, but the local organic product from the independent grocer seems more healthful and supports small businesses.

And what brand of jeans should we get? Jeans from the mall carry a smaller price tag than buying pants from a boutique . . . but is it a responsible purchase?

Just because something costs less doesn't mean someone else isn't paying the price for our savings. This is the difference between "cheap" and "costly" living. Living cheap can be easy and inexpensive yet may lack integrity. Living costly might ask more of us while forcing responsible and careful spending in order to avoid excess.

This same distinction can be applied to the Christian life.

In the New Testament, Romans 5 describes salvation as God's free gift to us, given while we were still sinners deserving death. That's grace. However, sometimes we become confused and focus on the "free" part of salvation and begin believing we deserve it. Dietrich Bonhoeffer calls this attitude "cheap grace."

In his book *The Cost of Discipleship*, Bonhoeffer writes, "Cheap grace is the preaching of forgiveness without requiring repentance, baptism without church discipline, Communion without confession . . . . Cheap grace is grace without discipleship, grace without the cross, grace without Jesus Christ."[1]

Cheap grace means ritual, not obedience. And compromise instead of conviction.

In direct contrast to cheap grace, Bonhoeffer challenges us to embrace costly grace. He says it "confronts us as a gracious call to follow Jesus, it comes as a word of forgiveness to the broken spirit and the contrite heart. Grace is costly because it compels a man to submit to the yoke of Christ and follow him; it is grace because Jesus says: 'My yoke is easy and my burden is light.' "[2]

There's a difference between living costly and living cheap. Are you up to the challenge?

—Robyn Roste

Endnotes

1. Dietrich Bonhoeffer, *The Cost of Discipleship* (London: SCM Press, 1959), 44–45.
2. Bonhoeffer, *The Cost of Discipleship*, 45.

Balancing the Work-Life Seesaw

On your feet now — applaud God!
Bring a gift of laughter,
sing yourselves into his presence.

Know this: God is God, and God, God.
He made us; we didn't make him.
We're his people, his well-tended sheep.

Enter with the password: "Thank you!"
Make yourselves at home, talking praise.
Thank him. Worship him.

For God is sheer beauty,
all-generous in love,
loyal always and ever.

~ Psalm 100 MSG

Stopping dead in my tracks, I gazed in wonder at the sunbeams cutting through the dense forest branches. I wasn't expecting to be caught off guard by this impressive scene. I drew a deep breath and paused to enjoy the moment. I realized how long it had been since I had the wherewithal to notice something so common as the sun and the trees and find them beautiful.

I'd been on a busy streak, wearing a lot of hats: wife, friend, homeowner, manager, daughter, sister, aunt, writer. My body had been telling me I need to be careful — that I was running on empty — but I was a bit lost on how to regain my work-life balance.

During that time, I attended a worship conference where the speaker reflected on a walk she took in the woods before the evening session. She said we can't get into creation without experiencing God, so if we're thirsty for more of His Spirit, then we should take a walk in nature, pause, look up, and pay attention to the Lord.

Such a simple idea, but I realized why my experience in the woods stayed with me: in my busyness I had taken a moment to be quiet, to get into nature, and I encountered the beauty of God's creation as a result. The lingering benefits I experienced were an uplifted spirit, a calmed mind, and a renewed sense of God's hand on my life.

The key to finding my balance between work and life is worship. While taking a day each week to attend corporate worship is essential and helps me focus on the Lord, I still need to find a way to weave worship into my daily life. Otherwise, I risk working in my own strength and forgetting to spend time in prayer. Otherwise, I risk working solely for the benefit of others and myself and not for the glory of God. Otherwise, I risk burning out.

Thinking about worship also helps me keep focused on why I work. In whatever I do, I want to cultivate a deeper relationship with God. In all aspects of my life, I want to serve the Lord and worship Him through my work. But I can't do that if I'm too busy to notice Him.

Here are five practical ways I've discovered to help achieve a work-life balance and keep my eyes focused on Christ.

1. Admit I can't do it all.

I used to pride myself on my multitasking skills, but when I began looking deeper into my productivity, I was surprised to see how much more I accomplished when I focused on one task at a time. I've also been pleased to notice how bumping tasks down the list or delegating them to others hasn't hindered their quality. When I admit I can't do it all, it's easier to let myself off the hook.

2. Implement boundaries.

Saying yes to people is one of my favorite things. I love helping out, pitching in, and doing favors. I love working. I find it fulfilling, enriching, and fun. Setting boundaries means I sometimes have to say no, which can be difficult at times. I've had to learn how to respect my own boundaries. Keeping boundaries in place is challenging, but the payoff brings me closer to achieving balance.

3. Prioritize tasks.

In university, I relied on lists to help me accomplish homework, research, and studying in the right order. When my professors handed out critical due dates, I'd plug them into my calendar and schedule my life for the next three months. But after university, I got out of the habit.

I realized school was pretty stress-free because my list told me what to do next. Therefore, I'm bringing lists back. While I no longer have exams, I do have lots to accomplish. Planning and prioritizing will help me get there in a balanced way.

4. Take time for relaxation.

Turning work off is hard. Relaxing is hard. Quiet time is hard. Sometimes I drive out to a place without cell service, so I won't be tempted to check in when I'm supposed to be taking a break. I've made a deal with myself to take time each week to get into nature and remain mindful of why I work and what my ultimate purpose is in life.

5. Pace myself.

Life is not a sprint. Sure, sometimes the pressure's on and I need to move fast, but I need to remember I can't always be going flat-out. Becoming more aware of my needs, priorities, and stamina has been important as I move toward a better work-life balance. And it's making my journey much more enjoyable as a result.

When my work-life is well-balanced, I feel good. The best way I can describe the feeling is that it's like receiving a well-executed high-five.

Anticipating a high-five used to stress me out — I'd see it coming and break out in a sweat. I'd wind up, swing my arm toward the waiting palm and . . . miss. Every time.

Until one day when I stumbled upon a piece of information that changed everything: **keep your eyes on the elbow**.

That's the key. Now, when I see the high-five coming, I keep my eyes fixed on the other person's elbow, and what do you know, it works.

Lots of simple tricks can make life a bit easier, and some tricks can change lives. The high-five secret is akin to the life-changing advice in Hebrews 12:2: **keep your eyes on Jesus**.

Here's the verse:

> *Do you see what this means — all these pioneers who blazed the way, all these veterans cheering us on? It means we'd better get on with it. Strip down, start running — and never quit!* No *extra spiritual fat, no parasitic sins. Keep your eyes on* Jesus, *who both began and finished this race we're in. Study how he did it. Because he never lost sight of where he was headed — that exhilarating finish in and with* God *— he could put up with anything along the way: cross, shame, whatever.* And *now he's* there, *in the place of honor, right alongside God. When you find yourselves flagging in your faith, go over that story again, item by item, that long litany of hostility he plowed through.* That *will shoot adrenaline into your souls!*
> (Hebrews 12:1–3 MSG)

Keeping your eyes on Jesus may seem too simple, but just like the high-five trick, if you know where to look, you won't miss. Hebrews 11 lists several heroes of the Bible who lived by faith — who "placed their hope in a better life after the resurrection" (11:35). It's the practical how-to guide to answer the question: How do I live by faith?

The writer of Hebrews compared the Christian life to a race — a marathon, really. I don't know what it is about marathons, but lately it seems like everyone I talk to has either recently participated in one or is training for one. Well, everyone except me. I jog regularly but only as a way to stay fit. Twenty-six miles of pain and suffering doesn't sound like a good time to me.

If not for the good time, why are so many people into marathons? For many people, crossing the finish line is one of the great accomplishments in life. With finishing as the goal of a marathon, it makes more sense why people would completely change their lifestyles and diet, endure injuries and pain, and persevere past the point when their brains shout, *Stop!* Because the goal is worth so much more than the cost of preparation and training, people endure the sacrifice.

In this context, the marathon analogy makes perfect sense. Why would anyone choose a life of discipline, sacrifice, pain, and suffering unless the goal was worth more than the cost? By placing our hope in a better life, we can see the finish line we're racing toward.

By admitting I can't do it all, implementing boundaries, prioritizing tasks, taking time to relax, and pacing myself, I'm able to achieve work-life balance. But when I'm in the thick of life and work, it's easy to lose sight of what I'm running toward. Keeping focused on why I do what I do keeps me motivated, productive, and willing.

Work-Life Balance: One Step at a Time

Everyone has a "thing."

You know . . . a thing you hate but your friends manage to convince you to do anyway, despite your better judgment.

A thing you can't usually motivate yourself to do.

My thing is running. Although I like it better now than I did a year ago, the inspiration to go for a jog still usually needs to come from outside sources, especially if the weather is cold and wet.

The other night after work is a prime example. My friend suggested running at the local track, but by the time I got home I sure didn't feel like it. Plus, it was miserable—cold and rainy and dark. And I didn't want to go.

Despite my reluctance we bundled up and went. As we drove over, I asked, "So how many laps were you thinking?"

"What about eight tonight?"

It's a good thing I was already sitting, because my legs felt weak. I wondered how I could possibly jog eight laps around a track when I didn't even know if I could step one foot out of the car.

As soon as we hit the track, my friend showed me a line and said, "This is our marker. Let's make it once around."

And after the first lap, she said, "Now, two."

We kept counting one lap at a time until, before I knew it, we finished eight. It's funny how much easier it is to run eight laps when we take it one lap (or step) at a time.

—Robyn Roste

The Deep Pit

If I say, "Surely the darkness will overwhelm me,
And the light around me will be night,"
Even the darkness is not dark to You,
And the night is as bright as the day.
Darkness and light are alike to You.

~ Psalm 139:11–12 NASB

I cried for forty days straight.

The birth of my first child should have been an occasion for unadulterated joy. He was healthy, beautiful, and we prayed for his arrival long before we knew for sure that I could get pregnant.

Instead, I wept, daily. The tears began before he was even born, really. When I was in the hospital being treated for premature labor. When I was on bedrest for two months. When I went into labor while my OB was on vacation, and the doctor who attended the birth argued with my husband over my laboring bed. She was frustrated that I didn't want to just get a C-section to get the birth over with. I sobbed, terrified, when that same OB eventually cut me open, and as I convulsed from the epidural's side effects, alone in a dark post-op room. I didn't touch, hold, or even see my baby boy for six hours after his birth.

I tried to keep up with the challenges of new motherhood and post-op recovery. I had trouble nursing, and I came home with my precious and ever-hungry baby without necessary pain medicine. My parents flew in to help, but my mother, who then believed that the world would be ending in a few months, refused to hold my son or bond with him for the entire visit. Instead, she voiced her disappointment that I had gotten pregnant. I spent my days doubled over in pain in the bathroom, the laundry room, and the kitchen, constantly reminded of my insufficient milk supply, feeling guilty for being unable to even feed my child. I felt increasingly isolated from my husband, with this intensely physical exhaustion and sorrow seeping into my skin and bones, infecting me with intense feelings of inadequacy and failure. I had no words, no energy to explain what was happening to me. Days blurred into nights with little sleep and no relief.

It was as if I were fighting to keep my grip on a balloon, grabbing desperately for the string in the middle of a storm, holding on to keep from falling.

The storm was too strong.

I couldn't hold on anymore.

The Pit

I fell into "The Pit" of depression. If you've been depressed, you know what it's like to be a prisoner in the pit. It plunges deep down into a place of thick anguish, paralyzing numbness, impenetrable darkness. Its walls are so terribly narrow; it feels impossible to move much less raise your arms to reach for help. It's a place where hope is blown away quicker than a balloon in a gale-force wind. The sound of rescue gets too muffled to perceive down in that pit. There is only sitting, silence, sadness, somberness, sleep.

If you have been depressed, you're not alone. According to the National Alliance on Mental Illness:

> An estimated 16 million American adults — almost 7% of the population — had at least 1 major depressive episode last year. People of all ages and all racial, ethnic and socioeconomic backgrounds can experience depression, but it does affect some groups of people more than others. Women are 70% more likely than men to experience depression.[1]

Depression is a pressing, present, pervasive mental illness. If it hasn't affected you personally, it *has* affected someone you love or someone you work or attend school with, and it has definitely impacted your church. Yet depression is at times considered a taboo subject, especially in our spiritual spaces, for two primary reasons. First, depression is insidious because it is invisible; it's an illness we cannot see without a trained eye. Second, admitting having depressive disorder can feel like an admission of failure rather than what it really is — a medical issue.

Christians Get Depressed Too

Many of us are trapped by the false impression that Christians who experience depression are somehow spiritually inferior, lacking in faith or maturity. After all, if we have the mind of Christ, how can we also be in need of mental healing?

This is the tension of the Christian life: we have been saved through Jesus Christ, yet we are still far from perfect — mentally, emotionally, spiritually, or physically (Romans 8:23). We remain vulnerable to physical maladies, emotional trauma, and mental illness on this side of the Lord's return. Rarely is a cancer patient chided with questions like, "So what did *you do* to develop that brain cancer? And what are you going to do to heal yourself?" Yet many of us ask the wrong questions and have unrealistic expectations of those who suffer from depression. Depression is not inherently a sin problem, it's an illness. Like many physical illnesses, depression can be caused by any number of combinations of internal and external factors — environmental toxicity, hormonal imbalance, diet, genetics — factors that those suffering with disease can do little to control or alter.

So yes, Christians *can* develop depression.

It's helpful for us to treat depression in the same way that Jesus treated the blind man in John 9. The disciples asked the wrong questions: "Rabbi, . . . why was this man born blind? Was it because of his own sins or his parents' sins?" (John 9:2). Jesus' answer silenced their line of questioning and shifted the focus to the Lord:

> *"It was not because of his sins or his parents' sins. . . . This happened so the power of God could be seen in him. We must quickly carry out the tasks assigned us by the one who sent us. The night is coming, and then no one can work. But while I am here, I am the light of the world."* (9:3–5)

When we or our brothers and sisters in Christ are suffering from depression, we can support them by helping them get out of the pit and into the light.

Depression in the Bible — It's in There

Though the word *depression* isn't a word used in most English translations of the Bible, it's a trait displayed by God's people — even those closest to God had bouts of depression.

Isaiah 53:3 describes Jesus as "despised and rejected — a man of sorrows, acquainted with deepest grief." Our *sinless* Savior was described in infallible Scripture as a "man of sorrows." Think about that. Jesus knew pain and loss (alternative translations for "sorrows"), disease and sickness (alternatives to "grief"). Imagine what Jesus must have experienced as the Creator, walking in the damaged aftermath of the fall, observing suffering, oppression, disease, death, and corruption. As He prayed in the garden of Gethsemane, Jesus said, "My soul is crushed with grief to the point of death (Matthew 26:38)." It's safe to say our Lord was in a depressed mood as He anticipated unspeakable suffering and the pain of separation from His Father—a sensation He had never known. Yes, Jesus *was* acquainted with sorrow and grief—and depression. To make their acquaintance, therefore, is not a sin. It's a hazard of living in a fallen world.

All through Scripture we can see the sorrow-inducing tension of knowing God's ideal and yet experiencing the by-products of the fall—a by-product of existing simultaneously as a citizen of God's kingdom and living in this fallen world, knowing and longing for God's ideal while living in a state where the ideal cannot yet exist. Here are a few snapshots of people in the Bible who most likely suffered from depression:

- **Job**, after experiencing the deaths of his family members and the loss of his livelihood, said: "I loathe my own life" (Job 10:1 NASB).
- **Leah**, after experiencing rejection by her husband and lingering dissatisfaction after bearing children to earn Jacob's love, stated: "The Lord has noticed my misery, and now my husband will love me" (Genesis 29:32).
- **Naomi**, after the deaths of her husband and sons, loss of her home, then returning to her hometown destitute, bereaved of security and family, and arriving with a foreign daughter-in-law, lamented: "Call me Mara, for the Almighty has made life very bitter for me" (Ruth 1:20).
- **Hannah**, after years of barrenness, cried so hard while praying that Eli the priest thought she was drunk: "I am very discouraged. . . . I have been praying out of great anguish and sorrow" (1 Samuel 1:15–16).

- **Elijah**, with the favor and power of God, after slaying Baal's false prophets (1 Kings 18), caved immediately when Jezebel threatened his life. He then ran away and asked to die: "I have had enough, LORD. . . . Take my life" (19:4).

- **David**, expressing depressive thoughts and lamenting about feeling forgotten by the Lord, proclaimed: "I am losing all hope; / I am paralyzed with fear" (Psalm 143:4).

- **Jonah**, angry with God for His mercy to Israel's enemies, fought God's directives and asked to die rather than witness His salvation: "Just kill me now, LORD! I'd rather be dead than alive if what I predicted will not happen" (Jonah 4:3).

- **John the Baptist**, despite leaping in his mother's womb on hearing his relative's voice (Luke 1:44) and being Jesus' cousin and forerunner (Mark 1:2–4) and being tasked with proclaiming the coming of Messiah (are you catching John's extensive faith pedigree?), had such deep doubt as he endured imprisonment and impending death that he asked Jesus, "Are you the Messiah we've been expecting, or should we keep looking for someone else?" (Matthew 11:3).

- **Judas**, as a result of unbearable remorse and guilt, flung himself into isolation and suicide: "I have sinned . . . for I have betrayed an innocent man" (Matthew 27:4).

- **Paul**, needing God's supernatural reassurance to press on (Acts 18:9–10; 23:11; 27:23–24), described his missionary journey to Asia: "We were burdened excessively, beyond our strength, so that we despaired even of life" (2 Corinthians 1:8 NASB).

What can we learn from these examples from the Bible? First, depression isn't new, and its symptoms are present in the biblical account. Second, depression occurred even in the lives of those committed to the Lord, so it shouldn't surprise us that it also affects Christians today.

What Is Depression? Clinical Hazard Signs

Let's get practical: everybody has a melancholy day once in a while, but what's the difference between the blues and depression? The most insidious aspect of depression is that it's not apparent unless you know the signs, and if there is not intervention, a depressive episode can alter a person's brain chemistry in as little as three weeks, impacting neurotransmitters and increasing the breakdown of serotonin — the feel-good hormone. Brain chemistry cannot be healed without serious intervention.

According to *DSM IV*, when a person presents with **five or more** of the indicators described below, in a given *two-week period*, he or she is diagnosed as having depressive disorder. If a person exhibits just *one* of the symptoms, however, he or she is diagnosed with depressed mood or loss of interest.

1. Depressed mood most of the day, nearly every day, as indicated by either subjective report (e.g., feels sad or empty) or observation made by others (e.g., appears tearful)

2. Markedly diminished interest or pleasure in all or almost all activities most of the day, nearly every day (as indicated by either subjective account or observation made by others)

3. Significant weight loss when not dieting or weight gain (e.g., a change of more than 5 percent of body weight in a month), or decrease or increase in appetite nearly every day

4. Insomnia or hypersomnia nearly every day

5. Psychomotor agitation or retardation nearly every day (observable by others, not merely subjective feelings of restlessness or being slowed down)

6. Fatigue or loss of energy nearly every day

7. Feelings of worthlessness or excessive or inappropriate guilt (which may be delusional) nearly every day (not merely self-reproach or guilt about being sick)

8. Diminished ability to think or concentrate, or indecisiveness, nearly every day (either by subjective account or as observed by others)

9. Recurrent thoughts of death (not just fear of dying), recurrent suicidal ideation without a specific plan, or a suicide attempt or a specific plan for committing suicide[2]

Seven Lessons from My Time in the Pit

Depression threatened to undo me, paralyzing my ability to even ask for help, robbing me of the joys that came alongside the challenges of new motherhood, and almost destroying my marriage. *But God.*

Today, by the grace of God and the grit of my loved ones, I have been pulled out of the pit and back into the light. I have a treasury of mistakes and hard-earned lessons about depression that I'd like to share with you.

- **Take a sober analysis of yourself.** We are all prone to short-term depression . . . *all of us*. The first way to counteract depression is to admit that it *can* happen. Family history, genetics, and stressors are among the risk factors that can elevate the risk of depression.

- **Pay attention to your circumstances.** Were you assaulted? Were you just laid off from work? Did you just adopt a child? Have you relocated recently? Have you had a break-up or divorce? Are you grieving the loss of a loved one? Experiencing an identity shift (graduating, getting married, promotion or demotion, career change, return to school)? The paths to depression are manifold. Examine recent events to discover what stressors, even happy circumstances, could trigger depression.

- **Self-care is not selfish.** It's not sinful to sleep, eat, laugh, or rest. God was so adamant about Sabbath rest that He incorporated it into the Law (Exodus 20:8 – 11). I was too prideful to accept help when I needed it most. If I could've had a do-over, I would have rested and allowed other people to burp my baby, scour the kitchen, fold the laundry, and enter into my mess. I would have taken more walks alone. I would have told my mom that I *needed* her.

- **Are you sleeping? How's your diet? Are you moving?** Sleep deprivation is a method of torture for a reason; humans need an average of seven or eight hours of sleep per night in order to feel rested. There are foods that boost your emotional health. Omega-3-rich foods such as wild salmon and sardines, vitamin D-rich greens, and tryptophan-rich turkey are natural supplements. Sometimes a visit to the pit can be roundly thwarted by healthy changes. Exercise boosts self-esteem and endorphins — the feel-good hormone.

- **When your instincts are dull, trust your friends and loved ones.** If the people you most trust are concerned about your mood, pay attention. Thank God for friends and spouses who care enough to share their concerns. Listen to them.

- **Don't even *try* to do this alone.** When you are depressed, you need help to pull you out. But you will *feel* like you are alone at the point when you need other people the most. Elijah felt that he alone stood as God's prophet, though there were 7,000 others in God's corner (1 Kings 19:10, 18). Every other observation I list are suggestions to *stave off* depression before it takes hold, but if you fall into the pit, you can't pull yourself up by your bootstraps. You cannot move, much less pull yourself out. You may feel needy or burdensome. Go ahead and feel the feelings *while you get the help you need.* When you are ill, pride must take a backseat to healing.

- **Pray.** David, well-acquainted with depression, wrote, "The sacrifice you desire is a broken spirit. You will not reject a broken and repentant heart, O God" (Psalm 51:17). Even in the brokenness of the pit, the Lord is near. He has a tender, gentle love when our spirits need tending. When we don't have the words to pray, the Spirit covers us: "The Holy Spirit helps us in our weakness. For example, we don't know what God wants us to pray for. But the Holy Spirit prays for us" (Romans 8:26). God is with you, even in the pit. And when you get out (and you will), you will trust Him in a more intimate way.

- **Counseling, medication, and professional help are your friends.** Sadly, in some Christian communities, any help besides prayer and Bible reading is considered negative. Though most of the same folks would think nothing of popping a Tylenol to deal with chronic pain, they wag their finger at popping a Zoloft. *You literally don't have time for these folks. Relentlessly pursue healing.* Talk with your primary care physician or OB/GYN. Ask your pastor for professional counseling referrals. If you can't make the call, have a trusted friend do the footwork for you and get you to your appointment. And if you are prescribed a pill, pay attention to your body and your emotions, and talk to your doctor about tweaking your prescription until you are out of the pit.

I thank God for the loved ones who carried me with their compassion and many, many prayers. I am grateful for the practitioners who listened and observed me carefully and set me on a path to physiological healing. Hope floated back to me. The Lord, through community and His patience and love, tied hope's string around my wrist. I know how to avoid falling back into the pit.

Still, I wince a little when life's harsh winds kick up.

I let brother Paul, who knew some dark times, speak to me through Romans 8:35 and 38:

> Can anything ever separate us from Christ's love? Does it mean he no longer loves us if we have trouble or calamity, or are persecuted, or hungry, or destitute, or in danger, or threatened with death? . . . I am convinced that nothing can ever separate us from God's love. Neither death nor life, neither angels nor demons, neither our fears for today nor our worries about tomorrow — not even the powers of hell can separate us from God's love.

—Sharifa Stevens

Endnotes

1. National Alliance on Mental Illness, "Depression," http://www.nami.org/Learn-More/Mental-Health-Conditions/Depression, accessed Apr. 25, 2016.
2. Mental Health Matters, in American Psychiatric Association on January 24, 2009: "Depression Criteria: DSM IV," http://mental-health-matters.com/depression-criteria-dsm-iv/, accessed Apr. 25, 2016.
3. "Reproductive Health: Depression and Postpartum Depression," Centers for Disease Control and Prevention, https://www.cdc.gov/reproductive-health/depression/pdfs/ppdchecklist.pdf, accessed Apr. 25, 2016.

Other Web sites used:
http://www.cdc.gov/mmwr/preview/mmwrhtml/mm5938a2.htm
https://www.cdc.gov/reproductivehealth/depression/pdfs/ppdchecklist.pdf

Depression Checklist[3]

The following checklist will help you start a conversation with your provider. Check the boxes that best describe your experience over the **past 2 weeks**, and take the checklist with you to give to your provider at your next visit.

In the past 2 weeks (14 days), how often have you:	A Few Days	Over Half the Days	Every Day
Felt sad or low?			
Felt more tired than usual, or have less energy during the day?			
Felt upset or annoyed at little things?			
Had trouble thinking, concentrating, or making decisions?			
Had no appetite or been eating too much?			
Worried that you might hurt yourself or felt like you wanted to die?			
Had trouble enjoying things that used to be fun?			
Felt like you have no one to talk to?			
Felt that you just can't make it through the day?			
Felt worthless or hopeless?			
Had headaches, backaches, or stomachaches?			

Complete the following questions only if you have given birth to a baby in the last 12 months.	A Few Days	Over Half the Days	Every Day
Had problems sleeping when your baby sleeps, or sleeping too much?			
Felt numb or disconnected from your baby?			
Had scary or negative thoughts about your baby?			
Worried that you might hurt your baby?			
Felt worried or scared that something bad might happen?			
Felt guilty or ashamed about your job as a mom?			

Pursuing True Health

"Peace I leave with you; My peace I give to you; not as the world gives do I give to you. Do not let your heart be troubled, nor let it be fearful."

~ John 14:27 NASB

What Is Biblical Wellness?

While waiting to have my annual physical, painfully aware of my aging body and the fatigue that I'm sure has hit an all-time high, I browsed through the magazines on the coffee table in the waiting room and quickly remembered why I steer clear of most magazines. Our culture's view of health and wellness screams from the covers, with skinny, air-brushed, designer-clad women who have it all together. It takes a lot of self-discipline to shut off the flow of thoughts of inadequacy after only glancing at a few magazine covers.

As believers we must ask ourselves: *What is true wellness? What does it really mean to be healthy?* Our culture provides many answers that leave us feeling overwhelmed — and if we're not careful, bankrupt! According to a May 2012 ABC News report, Americans spent $20 billion on diet books and diet medications and weight-loss surgeries.[1] Since then, however, with the resurgence of common sense, exercise, and eating fruit and veggies, the diet industry has taken a blow.[2] Could it be that people pursuing healthy lives have had enough of the quick-fix solutions that always fall short?

While our culture fails to provide the answers we're searching for, Scripture doesn't. In fact, God has a lot to say about *shalom*—the biblical concept of peace, characterized by a life of holistic health and wellness. As women fighting to swim upstream against the strong currents of cultural expectations, we need shalom. We need the profound peace of God to anchor us so we can live a life of full-orbed wellness.

My Story

For most of my early life, I struggled to achieve my perception of a "healthy woman" — a woman with a perfect body, an outgoing personality, a towering intellect, and the emotional stability that could withstand life's painful inevitabilities. For years, I have tried to live up to this idealized woman. I have always loved sports and exercise, and I have no problem fitting a workout into my daily schedule. But I have also always struggled to exercise self-control when it comes to food. As a result, I would often feel guilty eating if I didn't work out for hours first. In addition, because I am naturally shy, I dread being the center of attention. To compensate, I pursued physical perfection, but my lack of control over what I ate prevented me from achieving it. Deep down, the perception I had of a healthy woman and my inability to meet my self-imposed expectations were driving me to depression, which is the opposite of peace and biblical wellness.

It wasn't until well into my twenties, after a lot of prayer and spiritual maturing, that I began to rest in my identity as God's daughter and was able to find peace with who He made me. Finally, He enabled me to let go of many of my fears and inadequacies and begin to embrace His shalom.

Shalom for Women

After Jesus' crucifixion, while His fearful disciples huddled in a dark room, too scared to look out the windows or unlock the doors, perhaps they thought back to Jesus' words in the Upper Room as He prepared the disciples for their new life without Him. Knowing that anxiety and fear plague most people, and especially His disciples who would lead lives in direct contradiction to their culture, Jesus promised them — and us — *peace*. Not only would Jesus give His followers the promise of calm but also a *Person* — the Holy Spirit, the third member of the Godhead — whose residence in them would transform their entire being from the inside out. The indwelling Holy Spirit is the key to the peace and the holistic well-being we all seek.

As a woman, a wife, a mom, and a writer, I struggle to experience the true, deep peace that permeates every area of my life. Cultural expectations don't even come close to the unreachable expectations I have for myself. If my kids watch too much TV or eat too much candy or I miss my workout or treat my husband poorly, feelings of failure crowd out peace. But the indwelling Spirit offers grace and a profound sense of calm that surpasses busy schedules, habitual failures, and unrealistic cultural expectations. As the Spirit sanctifies us and makes us a little more like Jesus each day, He reminds us that our sins have been forgiven and that we have the power to make better choices next time (Romans 8:2). No one else can promise us this kind of peace! Jesus, however, wasn't the first to promise this kind of peace.

In the Old Testament, the goal of life was to achieve shalom, or wholeness, safety, and fulfillment. And the only source for the deepest level of shalom, the deep sense of calm that transcended Israel's circumstances, was God. As the Israelites stood at the edge of the Promised Land and received God's commands that would set them apart as His holy people,

Aaron the priest blessed the people with peace. Though Aaron spoke his benediction over Israel, we can apply some principles from his prayer to our lives today. Aaron's benediction in Numbers 6:24 – 26 illumines three aspects of God's shalom: God *defends* His people, *reveals* Himself to His people, and *acts powerfully* on behalf of His people.

First, the Israelites depended on God's promise to defend them from their physical enemies. As believers today, we depend on God to protect us from our spiritual Enemy. Fearing Satan will surely dispel our sense of shalom. Second, God revealed Himself throughout the Old Testament, but His self-revelation culminated with the advent of Jesus, who reconciles us with God and gives us eternal shalom. Third, Aaron prayed that God would *lift up His countenance* or act powerfully on behalf of the Israelites. When the priests offered sacrifices on the Israelites' behalf, they trusted that God would look favorably on the sacrifices and extend grace. As our great High Priest, Jesus has opened the floodgates of grace for us. We never have to wonder if God loves us or whether or not He wants to work powerfully in our lives.

Fear often drives our relentless pursuit of what the world views as *health*. Fear of rejection or the fear of being exposed as flawed women determines the way we spend our time and the kind of image we are painting for the world to see. But the biblical concept of shalom can flip our outside-in perspective of health to an inside-out view of true wellness.

Different Kinds of Health

When we think of health and wellness, our minds automatically think of exercise and healthful eating. But these are just the tip of the iceberg and may be even the least important aspects of true health. The Bible speaks of many aspects of health: physical, spiritual, emotional, relational, financial, and intellectual, but I'm going to focus on the intersection of physical and spiritual health. To neglect either of these aspects of health will lead to an imbalanced, unhealthy life.

Physical Health

Before we address spiritual health, which is the foundation of shalom, let's address a common misunderstanding in Christian circles. Many well-meaning Christians teach that our true identity is found in the immaterial part of us, that the "real me" is my soul. My body, on the other hand, is a prison to burst out of and to be liberated from at death. My body, therefore, isn't part of the "real me." So what's the problem with this view? The Son of God, the second member of the Trinity, became a man, complete with a physical body, which He retains even today! When Jesus rose from the dead in His glorified, recognizable body, He affirmed that His physical body was part of His identity. After His resurrection, the "real Jesus" is forever body and soul, material and immaterial. What astounding humility for the Son of God to take on our humanity and physicality for the rest of time!

Likewise, each of us is a body-soul combination, uniquely designed and loved by God. God aligned our DNA perfectly to make us exactly who we are. Before we can pursue physical health, we must accept our bodies just as we are, knowing that our hair color, body type, height, and even the characteristics we wish we could change are precious to our Father.

Once we have accepted our physical bodies as the instruments God has given us to glorify Him, then we can pursue physical wellness with a healthy attitude.

As stewards of our bodies, we should do everything we can to sustain our health so we can be better moms, wives, daughters, sisters, friends, and workers. Exercise shouldn't consume our time or thoughts, but we should incorporate activities to strengthen our hearts, muscles, bones, and bodies. The benefits of exercise can't be emphasized enough. Exercise improves mood, increases our immune response to sickness, helps to alleviate some symptoms of depression, and is fun! The easiest way to stick to an exercise routine is to find an activity you enjoy and even get a friend to join you.

Healthful eating should also characterize the lives of good stewards (1 Corinthians 6:19–20; 10:31). While we shouldn't be ruled by a list of prohibited foods and an overly strict diet (unless health issues require this), we should try to eat nutritious foods that will best fuel our bodies to carry out our many responsibilities well.

Personally, I try to eat whole foods and avoid as many processed foods as possible, but I do love the occasional cheeseburger, pizza, ice cream, and chips. In moderation, these foods make life fun! I have struggled with a love-hate relationship with food, and until recently, I had little or no self-control when it came to food. This is where my pursuit of physical health requires a strong foundation of spiritual health and self-discipline.

Spiritual Health

Spiritual health starts with a saving relationship with God through Jesus and complete trust in God's sovereignty. So how can we become spiritually healthy? I have come to the realization that my spiritual health is dependent on how much time I commit to pursuing it. As a working woman and mom of two kids, time is a precious and illusive commodity! But if I want to be a loving wife, a selfless mom, and an effective writer, I *must* spend time on my spiritual well-being, learning to hear and follow the voice of the Holy Spirit. And pursuing spiritual disciplines is a great way to do that. Here are a few spiritual disciplines that can help us live with shalom and true health.

- *Solitude*
If I don't schedule time with God, the business of the day will fill in every single second. As a morning person, I get up earlier than my husband and kids so I can spend time alone with God. Even a few minutes gives me the clarity and focus I need to tackle the day. I try (very imperfectly) to view the Bible as a means to intimacy with God, not something to check off my list.

- *Silence*
Life can be very loud, so we must remove noisy distractions that we might hear from God. During my morning time with God, I try to intentionally sit quietly for a few minutes to listen. Sometimes I write down the anxious thoughts that cause internal noise and threaten my peace. I also try to keep the radio off when I'm driving alone.

- *Fasting*
I admit it. I don't like to skip meals! I love to eat, and depriving my body of nourishment for an entire day or more makes me nervous. Nevertheless, fasting provides an opportunity for women to find true nourishment from the Lord Himself. The pain of an empty stomach reminds us to depend on God to fill us with His peace. We can also fast from other things that steal our attention from God. For me, as difficult as fasting from food is, it's even more difficult for me to fast from exercise! (Before fasting from food, consult your medical doctor.)

- *Frugality*
When the commercials tell me that I can find peace in following the latest clothing trends, no matter how devastating those trends can be on my bank account, the discipline of frugality teaches me that a simple, focused

life provides peace. Before making a new purchase, practice frugality and choose either to go without or pick a cheaper alternative that will meet our basic needs.

- *Sacrifice*
  The Bible clearly commands us to set aside a portion of our income for God. But sometimes God asks us to exercise the spiritual discipline of sacrifice by giving of our money and time even beyond what seems reasonable, in order to remind us of our dependence on Him and His faithfulness to provide. God gives me so much joy when I give sacrificially and much peace as I learn to rely on Him.

- *Meditation*
  I believe that meditation on God's Word is the key to experiencing true holistic wellness. When we ground our minds and anchor our hearts in Scripture, the Spirit gives us peace and contentment even in the midst of trying circumstances. Meditation connects us to God's thoughts on our spiritual and physical health, and unifies the often chaotic components of our lives under His sovereign care.

- *Worship*
  When I get wrapped up in myself — *my* needs, *my* desires, *my* unfulfilled expectations — my shalom is sure to suffer. But the surest way to shift my focus from myself to the Lord is by practicing worship. It takes discipline to worship on a daily basis.

- *Prayer*
  Independent, go-getter-type women tend to take on the world without asking for help. God, however, designed us to carry out the tasks of life armed with His power. Prayer is the key to tackling life the right way, in

dependence on the Lord. The discipline of prayer (especially *listening* to God) also gives us access to our Father's desires for us and deepens our intimacy with Him, which results in profound calm as we carry out each task in His presence. I find that if I don't set aside time to pray and listen, distractions flood my life and wash away focused times of prayer.

- *Fellowship*
  I know how busy life can get! With two active kids, an energetic husband, work, a house to keep clean, and the desire to cook nourishing meals, adding one more thing to the schedule can send me into a panic. But fellowship with other believers is essential to my emotional and spiritual health.

- *Confession*
  Throughout each day, especially as I attempt to be a kind, patient mom, I'm reminded that I'm a sinner to the core. Each day, I shoot prayers heavenward such as: "*Lord, forgive me for . . .*" "*yelling at my son . . .*" "*biting comments to my husband . . .*" "*cruel thoughts . . .*" "*self-pity parties . . .*" But regular, focused times of confession give me time not just to get sin off my chest but to receive God's grace and forgiveness. As often as we become aware of sin in our lives, let's confess it to the Lord and to those we have offended.

What Now?

The last thing I want to do is add more to-dos to your already packed schedule. But as women who seek shalom and holistic health, let's revisit the spiritual disciplines above. If we want peace to characterize our lives and wellness to permeate our being, we must commit to practicing these disciplines on a regular basis. Here are some passages of Scripture to meditate on and some possible activities to do as we seek to incorporate spiritual disciplines into our lives.

Solitude, silence, and prayer: Read Matthew 14:22–23. Learn from Jesus who, even as the Son of God, set aside time alone to pray and listen to His Father. Schedule time alone with God each day when you are most focused and awake.

Fasting: Read Acts 13:1–3. When the early church leaders faced big decisions or trials, they fasted as they sought God's guidance. We should also practice dedicated times of fasting in order to discern God's will in certain circumstances or to address areas of sin in our lives. When was the last time you fasted? Are you facing decisions for which you need God's direction? Set aside a day to fast from food or something else that takes up your time and thought.

Frugality and sacrifice: Read Philippians 4:10–13 and 2 Corinthians 9:6–8. The key to practicing the disciplines of frugality and sacrifice is the characteristic of contentment. When we learn to accept not only God's provision but the circumstances He allows in our lives, we begin to depend on Him for our security, not on material things. What financial needs can you meet in your church or community that will help you rely on God?

Meditation and confession: Read Daniel 9:1–23. Often when we spend time reflecting on Scripture and on the attributes of God, we come face-to-face with our own depravity. This week, set aside some time to meditate on a verse or an attribute of God, and also to confess sin. And as Daniel sought God's forgiveness on behalf of Israel, we also ask for God to open our family members' eyes to their need for grace.

Worship: Read Psalm 96. When I remember and proclaim God's attributes, His glory, holiness, justice, grace, power, and so on, my outlook begins to transcend my shallow, selfish concerns. I love to read the psalms and listen to great hymns as a way of offering praise and adoration to God. We can also keep a worship journal to record God's mighty deeds in our lives.

Fellowship: Read Acts 2:42 – 47. True fellowship with other Christ followers requires personal sacrifice, long-term commitment, and hands-on involvement in the messy lives of others. And it requires us to let others see our struggles and scars. But the rewards of this spiritual discipline will fill our lives with joy, meaning, and love.

Do I still struggle with finding balance as I pursue physical and spiritual health? Yes. Will we as women always struggle to live with shalom, perfect wholeness, and well-being? Yes! Why? Because we live in a fallen world. But as we take steps toward biblical health and wellness and share our experiences with others, our lives will increasingly be characterized by peace, joy, and contentment in the Lord.

Sample Health and Wellness Calendar

Create a biblical health and wellness calendar incorporating spiritual and physical disciplines. Here's an example:

	Monday	Tuesday	Wednesday	Thursday	Friday	Saturday	Sunday
Spiritual Disciplines	Extend prayer time.	Study a passage of Scripture.	Meditate on one verse.	Fast from food or something else that grips your heart.	Spend five minutes in silence.	Write down the prayers God has answered.	Praise God for three of His attributes.
Physical Disciplines	Exercise.	Go for a walk.	Cut out sweets.	Exercise.	Take a nap.	Take time to stretch and relax.	Eat more fruits and veggies.

—Malia Rodriguez

Endnotes

1. "100 Million Dieters, $20 Billion: The Weight-Loss Industry by the Numbers," May 8, 2012, ABC News, http://abcnews.go.com/Health/100-million-dieters-20-billion-weight-loss-industry/story?id=16297197, accessed Sept. 6, 2016.
2. John Kell, "Lean Times for the Diet Industry," Fortune.com, http://fortune.com/2015/05/22/lean-times-for-the-diet-industry/, accessed Sept. 6, 2016.

The Trouble with Expectations

Here is the conclusion of the matter:
Fear God and keep his commandments,
for this is the duty of all mankind.

~ Ecclesiastes 12:13 NIV

We are not defined by the world's standards, our neighbor's standards, or even our own standards. The Lord alone defines our worth, and His love is not conditional.

Ethan and I, married for a little more than a year, sat among a diverse group: two middle-aged couples (their children grown and out of the house) and another young couple about to embark on the wedded journey. The conversation informally turned into each married couple offering advice for the bride- and groom-to-be. Eventually, everyone turned and looked in our direction, and I could tell it was our turn to share our limited marital wisdom as well as our greatest struggle from that year. I paused. As any married woman can tell you, there's no lone nugget of advice. Thankfully, Ethan answered first, mirroring my thoughts exactly: "One of our greatest frustrations has been expectations."

Prior to marriage, I had lived life oblivious to my struggle with expectations — those things we hope and plan for. But only a few months after saying "I do," with endless to-do lists and expectations flooding our lives, I could no longer ignore it.

I'm not sure which instance brought me full awareness . . . it might have been the time I panicked because Ethan cooked the eggs a different way than I had expected or when the wrecked tanker truck blocked my route home and pushed back our schedule several hours. Each day I would scramble to fit it all in: a full day of work, a four-mile jog, a trip to the grocery store, a call to out-of-state family, a gourmet spread for Ethan, time spent in God's Word. I was frustrated and often found myself in tears.

It couldn't be that I was doing too much — hadn't women been juggling the responsibilities of married life for millennia? Meanwhile, my mini-meltdowns over cakes that didn't quite bake and wrong turns in new areas of town were the symptoms of a life overwhelmed by expectations.

I have since learned I am not alone.

We all expect *something*. Women in particular tend to have a great deal of high expectations. We place expectations on others. Others place expectations on us. Our self-expectations determine what we pursue, define our understanding of success, and influence our self-image. Although helpful for providing structure and initiative, expectations often cause more harm than good.

So, what are we supposed to do about these expectations? If we can't get rid of them, how do we live with them?

What Is True?

In order to live with expectations, believers must base our lives in truth.

Truth is tough to find. The American do-it-yourself mentality says we can create our own reality with the right to-do list or equipment. Social media outlets allow users to manipulate and craft their identities, and as we peruse the Internet, we see that other women are everything we're not. A woman can post photographic proof that she has it all—husband, successful career, happy children, spacious and well-decorated home, and multiple hobbies—and can do it all while wearing high heels and an up do. Influenced by external pressure and with a pinch of comparison, we expect (or at least I sometimes do) that we also can have and do it all.

However, no amount of forethought or planning will allow us to be and do *everything*. (And realistically, I can't do *anything* in high heels.) The truth is, most of those pins we see on Pinterest didn't pan out for other pinners either. (For proof, conduct a quick Web search for failed Pinterest projects.) The expectations of this woman-eat-woman world usually only add to the stress and worry most of us already fight against.

Through the culture's eyes, a former executive turned stay-at-home mom lacks ambition, and a wife who selflessly serves her husband is a doormat. But thankfully, the culture's "pinned" standard for success doesn't match God's. In 1 Corinthians 1, the apostle Paul explained the wisdom of God which juxtaposes that of the world. God uses the foolish things of the world to bring Him glory.

The ultimate example of wisdom in God's economy is the plan of salvation. We serve a God whose Son was crucified for *our sins*. The world considers foolish not only this example of Christ's humility but also those who follow Him. "For indeed Jews ask for signs and Greeks search for wisdom; but we preach Christ crucified, to Jews a stumbling block and to Gentiles foolishness" (1 Corinthians 1:22–23 NASB). God did not choose us because of our vocations, home-decorating skills, or worldly successes. In love, God chose us for His glory.

We do not boast in our own achievements; we have worth through the work of Christ Jesus. "But by His doing you are in Christ Jesus, who became to us wisdom from God, and righteousness and sanctification, and redemption, so that, just as it is written, 'Let Him who boasts, boast in the LORD'" (1 Corinthians 1:30 – 31 NASB). It's easy to base our expectations on the images we see posted to social media, but we must resist the urge. We are not defined by the world's standards, our neighbor's standards, or even our own standards. The Lord alone defines our worth, and His love is not conditional (Romans 8).

When we feel the pressure of expectations, we must ask ourselves, *What is true? Do my expectations reflect God's wisdom or the world's?* In order to live with expectations, we must base our lives in truth.

Afraid to Fail

In order to live with expectations, believers must accept that God's plan is greater than our failures.

Ethan and I discovered early in our marriage that our unmet expectations communicated one thing: failure. Failure is shamed by culture, and we shy away from it to avoid humiliation. Disappointment and failure often leave us wondering if God notices our problems and pain.

Failure isn't a new concept, though. The Bible doesn't present a group of men and women who lived without regret or mistakes. Most of the characters we admire committed grave errors and blundered through different phases of their lives. Although Romans 8:28 is often given as the Christian cure-all, consider it in the context of failure:

> *And we know that God causes all things to work together for good to those who love God, to those who are called according to His purpose.* (NASB)

This *doesn't mean* we will never face difficulties, accomplish everything we start, win every race, and enjoy every moment of the ride. This *does mean* God has a good purpose for every event in our lives. Not *our* good purpose, but *His* good purpose. God doesn't promise to reveal His purpose for us, but we can trust He has one.

In Scripture, this principle is evident in Exodus 5. After years of Israelite enslavement to the Egyptians, God sent Moses to Pharaoh to demand the Israelites' release. After Moses and Aaron spoke to Pharaoh, it was clear Moses was hoping to have the slavery issue wrapped up in a day. But Pharaoh not only rejected Moses' request to free the people, he increased the Hebrews' work and misery. Moses must have wondered why God bothered bringing him to Egypt only to fail on day one. But would the Hebrews have longed for the land God promised if Pharaoh had poured wealth and luxury over them? Would they have been eager to leave if Egypt offered comfort and peace? Of course not! The hardships the Hebrews faced made Egypt an unpleasant home — driving them to yearn for their beloved Promised Land.

Failure isn't only a consequence of sin or product of poor choices. Moses obeyed God faithfully, but he returned home as an apparent failure. Even when the outcome differs from our expectations, we can trust God has a purpose in it.

As a woman, I am hardwired to fear my failure. What woman wants to fail? But God has a purpose for my failure, and it's one I can rely on. Although expectations tell us we can accomplish everything, the grace of God reminds us we never will. To live with our expectations, we must learn to accept that God's plan is greater than our failures.

Expectations and Contentment

In order to live with expectations, believers must serve God with joy and learn to be content.

Although Ethan and I have been married for nearly two years, I remember how our fifteen-month engagement seemed to span a lifetime. After Ethan's proposal and a short week announcing our news, wedding plans took over our lives. Like most expectant brides, I looked forward to marriage — the joy of my husband's companionship and the beginning of our joint lives.

But sometime in the middle months of our engagement, my joy sagged under the weight of wedding details. I began to feel the day would never arrive. I have never liked party planning, and I soon longed to talk about something other than table centerpieces, dinner menus, invitations, dress colors, and special music options. I dreamily longed for the next season when we would no longer be under the shadow of wedding plans . . . as if marriage is free from responsibility. (No stage of life is.) I had fallen prey to a falsehood of expectations: the "grass is greener on the other side" fallacy.

As Nancy Leigh DeMoss writes, "The Truth is, if we are not content within our present circumstances, we are not likely to be happy in any other set of circumstances."[1] It didn't take me long to recognize my unhealthy discontentment, and thankfully my wedding planning "doldrums" didn't last. The remaining days before our marriage were some of the most joyful in my life. But the short phase in the middle of my engagement proved that, even during joyful times, I can let the stress of my circumstances overwhelm my contentment. Only by God's grace can I find contentment in *all* circumstances.

We find this struggle with contentment in Scripture too. King Solomon was one of the wisest and wealthiest men in history. Rulers during his time came to Israel from far away to marvel at Solomon's splendor. But at the end of his life, Solomon didn't tout the importance of riches; he even hesitated to place great significance on wisdom. In the book of Ecclesiastes, we get a glimpse into the life of the man who had it all.

People generally envy success and wealth, but Solomon's continual refrain throughout the book of Ecclesiastes is, "Meaningless! Meaningless! . . . Everything is meaningless" (Ecclesiastes 1:1 NIV). He considered his wealth, wisdom, and work as nothing—apart from the joy that God provides in them.

Expectations often reveal our idea of success—and we associate success with happiness and contentment. But at the end of his life, Solomon (one of the rare few who probably achieved his expectations) found no lasting joy in material things. "When good things increase, those who consume them increase. So what is the advantage to their owners except to look on?" (5:11 NASB). Clearly, contentment does not follow the accumulation of possessions. Solomon found some satisfaction in quality relationships and daily faithfulness (9:7–9), but he proclaimed that ultimate purpose is found in serving God.

> *Here is the conclusion of the matter:*
> *Fear God and keep his commandments,*
> *for this is the duty of all mankind.*
> (12:13 NIV)

We can strive as much as we want, but it is all meaningless in the search for peace and contentment. God has already given us what we need: He has given us Himself. In order to live with our expectations, we must serve God with joy and learn to be content.

Living with Expectations

Ethan and I have been learning to live unafraid of our expectations. With our hopes rooted in truth, we can move forward with confidence in our decisions. With a God greater than our failures, we can trust His plan for the future. With the knowledge that only God — not our fulfilled expectations — can supply happiness, we can serve the Lord with joy and be content in whatever circumstance.

When I feel overwhelmed by the demands of marriage or life, it helps me to remember the exhortation our pastor gave Ethan and me on our wedding day:

> Marriage is not the beginning of a lifelong search to find significance, happiness, and meaning in marriage and everything that you do under the sun. Today you are completely aware that your life and marriage have significance, joy, and meaning, and you have found these things not under the sun but in the Son, that is the Son of God.[2]

Seasoning Our Words and Actions

Many times we don't realize we have expectations until they go unfulfilled. These unmet expectations can incite discontentment and frustration, both with ourselves and others. Whatever the situation, our response is our responsibility. Refrain from bouts of impatience or anger. Be patient with others and yourself. As Paul said, "Let your speech always be with grace, as though seasoned with salt, so that you will know how you should respond to each person" (Colossians 4:6 NASB). If you are a believer, the Holy Spirit is at work in you and making you more in the likeness of Christ.

—LeeAnna Swartz

Endnotes

1. Nancy Leigh DeMoss, *Lies Women Believe and the Truth That Sets Them Free* (Chicago: Moody Publishers, 2001), 220.
2. Andrew Voelker, wedding sermon for Ethan and LeeAnna Swartz, May 25, 2014.

Hope for the Hopeless Romantic

Promise me, O women of Jerusalem,
by the gazelles and wild deer,
not to awaken love until the time is right.

~ Song of Songs 2:7

I remember my first crush . . . Jason. He was perfect: velvety brown skin, bright smile, and able to burp the alphabet . . . he had the largest collection of Garbage Pail Kids cards and, therefore, the respect of the boys. And unbeknownst to him, he had my heart. I would stare at Jason during class between spelling exercises and watch as his huge, grey glasses trained on his paper. So studious. At recess, I would be skipping rope or playing tag with my girls on the outside, but on the inside, my heart skipped a beat every time I caught a glimpse of him in the schoolyard.

Jason, I thought, *you are so dreamy. One day, you will be my husband, and we will have two children and live in a big brick house and have a dog named Puddles, and she will be a poodle because you will let me choose, and you can burp the alphabet every night at dinner so our children can learn how to do that too.*

Did Jason know of my ardent devotion to him? Did he even care? Um, no. And the next year, he moved away, out of New York and out of my life, shattering my eighteen-year plan to go from schoolmate to bride.

Now, let me say, I am *mortified* that second graders are even capable of crushing on someone because that means my oldest son may have his heart skip a beat for his own crush in less than two years. (WHAT?!) That said, there's this thing in the vast majority of us . . . this longing to be swept away by overwhelming feelings that can only be described as *romantic* love.

Boy meets girl. Boy woos girl. Boy prepares elaborate expressions of love to win the girl's heart and hand in marriage. Boy and girl live happily ever after.

Is that romantic, or what?

What do you think of when you hear the word *romance*? Passionate kisses in the middle of a rainstorm? Love winning against all odds? Faithfulness through thick and thin, be it poverty or cancer or dementia?

The Creation of Romance

Romance in God's Word isn't anything like *The Notebook* or *Romeo and Juliet* — and aren't we grateful? — but that doesn't mean it's boring.

God wrote the Book when it comes to love, but He didn't just write the Book; He *is* love (1 John 4:8). We see this demonstrated most profoundly in His glorious Son, Jesus Christ — God's ultimate answer for humankind's sinful rebellion. Yet the Bible brims with countless other examples of God's love. When we consider the care He took in creating a world for us, in fashioning humanity in His image, and in designing a satisfying, exciting relationship for both Adam and Eve, God's delight and love for us is undeniable.

The book of Genesis dives into the first romance right after God's creation of the world — almost as if the narrative of creation couldn't be communicated without laying the framework of romance between the first man and woman. Adam and Eve's romance was built on *absence*, *longing*, *devotion*, and *fulfillment*.

Absence

As Adam diligently worked, encountering and naming each of the animals in earth's incredible menagerie, he discovered no one else like him. Adam lived in Eden — Paradise — and he, along with the entire world, was a stranger to sin. And yet . . . he was alone . . . and he *felt* it. And *God Himself* said, "Yeah, that's no good" (Genesis 2:18, my paraphrase). God created all the other animals with their mates, but even before Eve entered into the picture, Adam and God felt her absence.

Longing

Eve's absence from Adam's life, his lack of community, lack of partnership and likeness, created longing in Adam: "But for Adam there was not found a helper suitable for him" (2:20 NASB). Before God put all the animals on parade, He had purposed that He would *make* a companion for Adam. Adam wasn't in on God's plans, according to what is recorded in Scripture. Perhaps the Lord wanted to develop Adam's longing so that his appreciation of her would be heightened.

Devotion

When Adam met Eve, his excitement and joy were immediate, unfettered by pride or fear. There's a reason that Genesis 2:23 is indented in our Bibles — Adam was moved to recite the world's first poem: "At last! This is the one who is suitable to me! My companion is here, and she's perfect for me! Come here, woman!" (my paraphrase).

Fulfillment

The first romance was a runaway success, crafted by God. "Now the man and his wife were both naked, but they felt no shame" (Genesis 2:25). Imagine that: a romance with full acceptance and zero insecurity. A confident, bold love. An equal-opportunity vulnerability and openness. A love fully blessed by God.

Romance . . . Is This a Thing in the Rest of the Bible?

A popular book circulating in my young adulthood was *I Kissed Dating Goodbye*. This book, written by a young, single, Christian man, became a dating bible for many a youthful believer who, like me, struggled to figure out what, if any, dating rituals were endorsed by the Lord. The *Goodbye* book gave me all the answers I needed: don't date at *all*, it said. Meet in groups. Of course, no sex is allowed but also no kissing, hand-holding, intense individual attention . . . nothing. If, during the course of group "dating," I zeroed in on a special someone, his parents and my parents would all get together and decide whether it was a good idea to start "courting" — intentional dating with marriage as the ultimate destination.

There it was, the answer I had been looking for! After all, the Bible itself was written in an era when dating was a completely foreign concept, and arranged marriages were the rule. The Bible couldn't possibly inform dating. The Bible kissed dating goodbye too. Right?

Um, wrong. *Wrong*.

One of the things that encourages, frustrates, and challenges me the most about the Bible — and the God who inspired it — is that it refuses to be reduced to formulas and squeezed into teeny, tiny boxes.

When it comes to romance, the Bible is short on prescriptions and long on variety. In addition to the creation of the first couple, the Old Testament features several stories that highlight more than one formula to achieve a God-blessed union. For example, the sixty-seven verses of Genesis 24 portray the budding romance between Isaac and Rebekah in more detail than it describes the *entire* creation account.

Their love story began during a time of mourning. The death of Isaac's mother Sarah prompted Abraham to think of his son Isaac, who was lonely and longing and mourning his mother. Neither Isaac nor Rebekah knew that marriage was on the horizon, but the faith and action of a concerned father and the providence of God orchestrated the couple's union. By the time Abraham's servant went on his search for Isaac's bride, Rebekah had already established an instinctive practice of hospitality and strength (drawing water for thirsty camels takes more stamina than a CrossFit session) (Genesis 24:18–19).

When Rebekah discovered the servant's reasons for visiting her family's compound, she had a choice to make: Would she leave her home and family to marry a man whom she had never met, or would she stick with the familiar and ignore the signs of providence? Rebekah dove right into commitment to her soon-to-be groom when she said three little words: "I will go" (24:58).

Although arranged marriages may not be a part of modern-day Western culture, we can certainly relate to the *devotion* involved in leaving the familiar in order to commit to one's spouse. Rebekah demonstrated bravery and faith in submitting to God's providence, and God rewarded her — as soon as she first laid eyes on Isaac, she was drawn to him (24:64). What got Rebekah off her camel? Was it Isaac's meditating in the field, submitting himself to the same God who moved her to leave, or was it physical attraction that caused her to lift up her eyes and dismount her camel? I like to think that God rewarded Rebekah's bravery in betrothing herself to Isaac by fulfilling the desires of her heart *and* eyes . . . as the couple could still be seen making out years later, according to Genesis 26:8.

Rebekah, a young Israelite virgin, had little in common with Ruth — a Moabite, childless widow — yet the Lord's lovingkindness and providence was written all over her story as well. Ruth and her mother-in-law Naomi both felt the keen absence of the security that only a husband and children could bring in ancient Near Eastern culture.

Like Isaac and Rebekah, Boaz's admiration for Ruth was kindled in the fields, sparked by a single question: "Who is that young woman over there?" Boaz was struck by Ruth's presence immediately (Ruth 2:4 – 5), but his admiration grew dramatically when he discovered her robust work ethic (2:7) and her selfless devotion to Naomi (2:11) and to God (2:12).

But when Ruth brought home a generous amount of barley from Boaz's fields, Naomi began to glean hope that redemption was possible for her family. Ruth didn't exactly "kiss dating goodbye" when she sought — in a plan created by Naomi — to spend time lying at Boaz's feet, alone, late at night, at the threshing floor (3:1 – 5). Where Abraham's servant pursued Rebekah, Ruth pursued Boaz.

Boaz, impressed that Ruth would choose devotion to him rather than a younger man, was on a mission to redeem (3:10 – 11) — and all the while, he praised her (3:11), protected her (3:14), and provided for her (3:15). What a man!

Boaz's ability to discern Ruth's character, rather than just her status as a foreigner, and Ruth's faith-fueled pursuit of a man of noble character make them both praiseworthy.

With the examples of Adam and Eve, Isaac and Rebekah, and Boaz and Ruth, romance isn't characterized by candlelit dinners and heart-shaped chocolates, but a singular devotion and deep fulfillment in the midst of gritty, real-world absence and loss, comfort and joy. In other words, their stories are about real love in real life.

Sex and Romance

Let's be honest — when we hear the word *romance*, often we think of stolen glances and butterflies, electric touches and dynamite kisses. Physical chemistry. Sexuality. Right?

To be clear: *romance is not sex*. Romance can and does exist outside of the realm of marriage, and one need not have sex to be romantic.

That said, sex is a vital part of marital romance — celebrated, mutually satisfying, God-blessed. God is not a prude. He is the creator of sex and sexual ideal for fulfillment, and we know this because of 1) the leaving and cleaving and becoming one flesh that describes marriage in Genesis 2:24; 2) the *whole* book of Song of Solomon; 3) the frank descriptions of sex and sexual adultery in the Bible (one cannot read Ezekiel 23 and think that the Bible doesn't speak plainly); and 4) to be really, *really* frank, physiological evidence.

Let's focus on Song of Solomon for a moment. This biblical book is an unabashed celebration of romantic love and sexual expression — and it gets right to it:

Kiss me and kiss me again,
for your love is sweeter than wine.
How fragrant your cologne;
your name is like its spreading fragrance.
No wonder all the young women love you!
Take me with you; come, let's run!
The king has brought me into his bedroom.
(Song of Solomon 1:2–4)

Well, alright now! Sections of Song of Solomon extol the beauty of the woman (4:1–11), the handsomeness of the man (5:10–16), the heightened expectation of becoming lovers, and poetic inferences about lovemaking ("entering the garden" as a euphemism for the man's entering the woman—4:16; 5:1; 6:2).

Let me repeat: *God is not a prude.* He created us to enjoy sexual love within the beautiful boundaries of marriage. He knows the power, the bonding nature, and the intimacy that sex provides. God says to married couples, "Go on, you crazy kids—have fun and enjoy yourselves!" And Song of Solomon is an ode to that heady, intoxicating, erotic love.

However, weaved within the breathless loveliness of Song of Solomon is a strong warning. In Song of Solomon 2:7; 3:5; and 8:4, the text adjures the daughters of Jerusalem to promise "not to awaken love until the time is right." Why? Because "love is as strong as death, its jealousy as enduring as the grave" (8:6).

We are a love-obsessed society with an adolescent sense of what love really means. These days, adults as well as boys and girls are being taught about sex through pornography, sexting, and hyper-sexualized media. These sources portray sex as a casual, biological act, like eating, rather than an exclusive, monogamous vehicle of emotion, passion, and connectedness. Sex has become profoundly torn from the bounds of marriage and mishandled as a clumsy tool to generate romance, all the while bearing the fruit of lust. As a result, many of us have ended up naked and very much ashamed — in polar opposition to the romantic ideal.

Romance . . . and the Long Wait

Not all of us have romance in our lives, for any number of reasons: we aren't in relationships; we're widowed; we're divorced; a bad breakup has left us skittish; our marriages are rocky; or we live in spit-up splotched yoga pants and a postpartum haze.

I'm not going to tell you that if you faithfully participate in church, read your Bible, and pray, God will bless you with romance. We cannot earn the right to romance. Romantic love is one of many kinds of gifts from God — and all of God's gifts are unmerited. We all know spiritually grounded, lovely people who are not in relationships, as well as certifiable, selfish people who have perpetual suitors. Romance is not a merits game. If it were, the apostle Paul and Jesus Himself would have had spouses. Romantic love is not required for salvation or sanctification, and — read this carefully — *not having romance in your life isn't a sign that God loves you less.* Absence and longing happened *before* the fall; it's part of the human experience, not punishment. No matter where we are in the relationship status spectrum, though, God's grace is sufficient and His presence is sure. He is with us in the struggle.

In that vein, I won't tell you that God's love is a great stand-in that will diminish your longing for sex, because any of us who've felt the ache for physical intimacy know that's not always true. Some of us experience the profound disappointment of missing out on the devotion and fulfillment of a marriage, and that stings.

God created romantic and erotic love in His infinite wisdom as a gift to humanity and to display the oneness of the Godhead through His image-bearers. However, marriage is far from an eternal institution. In eternity there will be no marriage and no one being given in marriage. We won't need institutions to reflect aspects of God's being, because we will behold Him, face to face — no interpretations, reflections, or symbols will be necessary. And in His presence, we will experience a holistic body/soul/mind/heart contentment that will never again feel unfulfilled. *Never again.*

God's love is unconditional, eternal, unchanging, and perfect; it is something holy — completely other to the concept of romantic love. Romantic love may last a lifetime, but God's love stands forever.

Romance . . . What It Is . . . and Ain't

The first romance was characterized by openness, vulnerability, commitment, and partnership. God has desired for His people to "leave and cleave" in a healthy manner since the days of Adam and Eve. God wants those of us blessed to be in romantic relationships to enjoy them! *But even more than this, God desires that His people reflect His love and character through the way we treat one another.*

Christian marriage reflects more than romance — after all, it's a symbol of the love that Jesus Christ has for His church (Ephesians 5:32). In the gospels, Jesus' love isn't one-size-fits-all. He called the long-isolated woman with the issue of blood, "daughter." He spoke frankly about the love life of the woman at the well. Jesus' love pardoned Peter with the threefold charge to feed His sheep. He hushed Thomas' doubts by allowing him to touch His wounds. Jesus loves attentively, individually, knowingly. He is responsive, thoughtful, and tender. Jesus is our guide of Christian love. **Romance, at its pinnacle, is fueled by *sensitivity to God and attentiveness to our spouse.***

If romance emerged when God created the first woman and presented her to the first man in a sinless Eden, then it could be said that the breakdown of romance began at the fall. Adam stood by, silently watching Eve pluck the forbidden fruit, and they both actively disobeyed God's command (Genesis 3:6). They then covered themselves (3:7) and hid from God in shame (3:8).

With the fall came the erosion of romance and the advent of the struggle. We see vestiges of the fall in our relationships today: "You will desire to control your husband, but he will rule over you" (Genesis 3:16). After the fall, Adam named his wife in the same way he named the animals (3:20), separating himself from her. The following short (but not exhaustive) list describes what romance is *not*.

- *It's not romance if it separates you from God.*
- *It's not romance if he doesn't support you with the truth.*
- *It's not romance if only one of you is willing to be vulnerable.*
- *It's not romance if you consider your bodies something to be consumed rather than something holy.*
- *It's not romance if he's just not that into you.*
- *It's not romance if either of you are cheating.*
- *It's not romance if he physically hurts you.*
- *It's not romance if he uses words to demean you.*

—Sharifa Stevens

Turning Fear into Faith

Even when I walk
through the darkest valley,
I will not be afraid,
for you are close beside me.
Your rod and your staff
protect and comfort me.

~ Psalm 23:4

When my first child was born, my fairly secure, controlled world was invaded by a set of fears I had never known. And not just easily extinguished worries about busy schedules, what to make for dinner, or how I would get all my tasks at work done. This new world of fear penetrated through the shallow waves of stress to the depths of dread that I wasn't prepared for.

When my husband and I brought home our tiny, precious, helpless son, it hit me. *I'm a mother! I'm responsible for the life of this sweet boy.* As many new moms know, fear invades our minds the first night we put our newborns to bed. We think, *Will my baby stop breathing while we sleep soundly? Did I feed my baby enough? Is my baby crying too much?* Needless to say, new moms often don't sleep soundly for *many, many* months after their little ones are born!

And when my newborn became a toddler, yet another set of fears took over. *Will my problem-solving boy figure out how to open the front door* (yes, he did!) *and wander out of the house and into the street* (thankfully, he has not — yet!)? *Will he fall in the bathtub and drown? Will he eat something new and go into anaphylactic shock and die? Will he contract a deadly disease?* And the list of fearful questions goes on and on. I remember many nights when, after collapsing in bed and closing my eyes, terrifying scenarios of what could happen to my boy would threaten my sleep and shake my peace.

At the core, my new world of anxiety revealed the feeble foundation of my faith. I wasn't sure I had the right answer to the most important question: *Is God really in control?* Most days I would answer, "Yes, God is in control!" And then the scary follow-up questions would inevitably come: *Would I really be able to handle His will, even if it included the realization of my greatest fears? Would I be able to join Job and worship the Lord if He chose to take away the people I love the most?* Reflecting on these questions pushed me beyond fear to issues of control, further from the most difficult place to reach: contentment and complete trust in God. On this battlefield — the battlefield of contentment — we will either win or lose the fight against fear.

From Fear to Contentment

Fear is a normal part of the human experience, even among Christians. On the healthy side, fear is a God-given ability to detect and deal with a dangerous threat. It's an internal warning system that alerts us if something is wrong, or could go wrong, and prepares us to respond. But when fear begins to disrupt life, drain spiritual and emotional strength, or cloud judgment, it's time to lean in and deal with it.

When a new mom has nightmares about the horrible things that could possibly happen to her child, her fear can become an insurmountable obstacle, a towering mountain range, keeping her from joy and contentment. And then, when she tries to fight off fear with attempts to control all of her circumstances, fear just wraps its tentacles tighter. In an effort to prevent all the possibilities that caused me terror, I thought if I just kept my son home, safe, away from any potential danger, he would be okay. But my feeble efforts to control the environment and surrounding circumstances did nothing to rid my heart of fear. In fact, to the contrary, controlling behavior adds fuel to the fire of fear.

So what's the alternative? Contentment. We *can* live with contentment—a pervading peace that comes from entrusting ourselves totally to God's sovereign control. Contentment says, with Job,

> *"I came naked from my mother's womb,*
> *and I will be naked when I leave.*
> *The Lord gave me what I had,*
> *and the Lord has taken it away.*
> *Praise the name of the Lord!"* (Job 1:21)

Contentment finds satisfaction and fulfillment in God alone and His mysterious purposes.

But how do we leave fear behind and pursue contentment? When fear jeopardizes our peace, when we feel paralyzed, we can lean in and take our overwhelming feelings to the Lord, trusting in His comfort. We must search God's Word and cling to His trustworthy character.

During those sleepless nights when dread kept me awake, I began using that time to pray and to face the possibility that God's will may include the realization of some of my worst fears. In those troubling times wrestling with God, I voiced my feelings to my loving Father and received His comfort.

I also shared my dread with one or two close friends who could identify with my fears. Doing so, I discovered that I wasn't the only one with these new-mom fears! So by the time my second child, a daughter, came along, I had grappled with some of my fears and learned more about trusting God. However, conquering fear is not a one-time victory; it's an ongoing battle.

When the pediatrician's office called after my daughter's newborn screening came back "abnormal," terror flooded my mind and spiraled into numbing worry. The nurse explained that my daughter might have medium-chain acyl-CoA dehydrogenase (MCAD), a metabolic disease that prevents the body from turning certain fats into energy. After that frightening phone call, I made the mistake of researching MCAD online, and worry turned to despair. As we waited for the results of further blood tests, I embraced my fear and prayed. After wrestling with God, I realized that even if she did have MCAD, we would be able to handle it by watching her diet very closely. Thankfully, the genetic testing showed that she is only a carrier for the disease. But as I held my baby girl close, waiting those ten days for the results to tests that were completely beyond my control, I learned a little bit about trusting God and finding contentment in whatever circumstances He allows.

David's Contentment

In addition to working through fear in prayer, I also spent lots of time reading the book of Psalms. I took comfort in David's struggle with paralyzing anxiety as he ran for his life from King Saul.

David's running led him and his men into hiding deep in a cave. One day, while secretly tucked away deep in the cavern, David's mortal enemy, Saul, happened to enter that same cave to rest. After running for years, fearing for his life as Saul hunted him, David finally had a chance to rid his life of terror once and for all. It seemed to David's men that God had delivered Saul into David's hands.

As David stood behind his foe, with sword in hand, David quietly cut off a bit of King Saul's garment — instead of Saul's flesh (1 Samuel 24:4). Rather than acting in fear and usurping God's rightful control of his life, David deferred to the Lord and refused to kill Saul, God's chosen king (24:6). David chose contentment. David chose to face his fear, loosen his grip on control, and entrust himself to God (24:15).

As we learn from David and his godly response to fear, it's important to see how David and Saul dealt differently with fear. While anxiety pushed David toward God, it drove Saul's relentless, murderous pursuit of David. The Bible traces Saul's fear of David and, more important, Saul's dread over losing control of his kingship.

- "Saul was then afraid of David, for the LORD was with David and had turned away from Saul" (18:12).
- "David continued to succeed in everything he did, for the LORD was with him. When Saul recognized this, he became even more afraid of him" (18:14–15).
- "When Saul realized that the LORD was with David and how much his daughter Michal loved him, Saul became even more afraid of him, and he remained David's enemy for the rest of his life" (18:28–29).

Fear invaded Saul's life because of his lack of trust in God. And as Saul's terror festered, it intensified his desire to control his circumstances, maintain his grip on power, and attempt to murder David. When fear doesn't drive us to fellowship with God and to deeper trust in Him, it will lead us to discontentment and devastating attempts to control our circumstances.

David's Trust

In Psalm 11, David's fear pushed him into God's arms. Though David felt exposed and naked before his foe's arrows, he found refuge in the Lord's sovereign control over his life. As David, the future king of Israel, fled from King Saul, he had nowhere to turn. Some of his friends counseled him to flee to the mountains. But David knew that only the Lord, the righteous King of Heaven, could provide refuge. David began his prayer by explaining his problem (Psalm 11:1–3) — the wicked aimed their murderous bows at him. Then he declared his trust in God's protection (11:4–7). Even when David's circumstances and feelings pointed to what seemed to him as God's inactivity, David had confidence in the Lord.

As modern-day readers of God's Word, we can look back and see that the Lord did protect David. And we can also read about our Lord Jesus who trusted in the Father when Satan tempted Him, when evil people persecuted Him, and when He faced death on our behalf. Christians stand in a long line of struggling people who trust in the God of refuge and depend on His comfort.

In Psalm 23, one of the most familiar psalms, David declared his trust in the Lord, even in the midst of evil and overwhelming fear. When the road before David twisted behind trees and dipped into dark valleys, he depended on God. He drew on his experience as a shepherd using a rod and staff to care for his sheep. A rod was a club used to chase away wolves, and a staff was a long stick with a hook used to pull sheep out of thickets and holes. David counted on his heavenly Shepherd to protect him from his enemies and rescue him from danger.

Christians today trust that same Shepherd. Because we are human beings with finite knowledge, the uncertain path before us can cause fear. We need a guide who not only knows the destination but can shield us on the journey. Our Good Shepherd, Jesus Christ, knows and loves His sheep. So even if our worst fears become reality, we can walk with confidence.

At times, due to no fault of our own, fear-inspiring circumstances seem set against us. If so, we can pray with David in Psalm 59. David wrote this psalm in the context of Saul's men pursuing and hoping to capture or murder him. On the run and with feelings such as any person might have, David wanted to see these pursuers punished. No doubt he would have happily taken up the mantle himself. However, David restrained himself out of respect for God's anointed, King Saul. Instead of lashing out with his sword at his pursuers, David called upon God to do the work for him — to judge his enemies. And like David, who showed supernatural restraint regarding his enemies, we must choose to do the same. We must not take the reins of control from our sovereign God who loves us.

What Now?

Even though our kids might no longer be newborns, we still fear for them. In addition to the terror that haunts moms when we wonder if sickness or preventable accidents loom in our children's future, other worries sound like this: *Will I be able to cut it as a mom? Will I have the physical, emotional, and spiritual fortitude to help my children weather the storms of life? Will they inherit my struggles, anxieties, and lack of trust in God, or will I pass on a realistic faith that chooses to believe in God's faithfulness even when the circumstances of life seem stacked against them?*

In spite of packed schedules that overwhelm us, what we really need is *more* time with God, even if it's only an extra ten minutes each day. We need Him to help us wrestle with our deepest, most desperate concerns. We need a trusted confidant — and sometimes a Christian counselor — who will listen to our anxious thoughts and point us to truth. We must saturate our minds with Scripture, conform to its truths, and choose contentment over control.

Reading and rereading David's psalms helped me face my fears. As a result of King David's years living as a fugitive, God's Word contains many psalms that give words to our anxious thoughts.

I know that fear may remain an acquaintance throughout my life. But I have a choice — I can exert all my energy trying to control my uncontrollable circumstances, or I can view fear as a catalyst, driving me to trust God. We don't know what joys or sorrows tomorrow holds. God may in fact allow our greatest fears to come true. But that doesn't change the truth that God is good. He will walk with us through valleys so dark that we can't see our next step. As we learn to entrust ourselves to God and choose to trust Him in all circumstances, we will begin to develop unshakable contentment and joy.

Personalizing Psalm 11

As you seek to let go of fear and control and to pursue contentment, grab your spouse or a close friend and use the guide below to personalize Psalm 11.

Read 1 Samuel 18–24. Try to put yourself in David's sandals and imagine what it must have been like to live as a fugitive, running for your life from the king and his army. Keep these thoughts in mind as you work through Psalm 11.

Read Psalm 11:1–3. Reflect on your current life. Write down some of the people, circumstances, and fears that make you want to run away or shut down emotionally and spiritually.

Read Psalm 11:4. Use a concordance and search for other Bible verses that refer to God in His temple or on His throne. On a 3x5 card, write down the verse references you found and summarize the truth you discovered in each verse. How do these verses change the way you view your fears?

Read Psalm 11:5–6. Reflect on God's just character and remember that if you have believed in Jesus for salvation, you are righteous in God's eyes. In love, the Lord examines your heart and wants to expose and resolve your fears. Often God will allow your circumstances to surface the terrors He wants to use to deepen your trust in Him.

Memorize Psalm 11:7. Pray that God would help you see Him at work in the midst of your fears, anxieties, and challenging circumstances. Ask your spouse or a close friend to commit with you to resting in God's sovereignty, embracing contentment, and waiting for Him to act instead of trying to control your uncomfortable circumstances.

—Malia Rodriguez

Repainting Our Self-Image

My frame was not hidden from You,
When I was made in secret,
And skillfully wrought in the depths of the earth;
Your eyes have seen my unformed substance;
And in Your book were all written
The days that were ordained for me,
When as yet there was not one of them.

~ Psalm 139:15–16 NASB

Self-Esteem, Self-Worth, and Self-Image

We all have painted a self-portrait — a portrait that reveals how we see ourselves — a portrait that may or may not accurately represent our strengths, weaknesses, and inherent worth. Try as we may, we can't change our view of ourselves by mustering up self-esteem. Self-portraits portray decades of thought patterns and experiences and thus take time to restore. And self-portraits, which capture our deepest notions of our worth, must be restored based on God's view of us.

Webster's dictionary defines *self-esteem* as "a confidence and satisfaction in oneself." In our self-help-focused culture, much of the talk about self-esteem encourages women to focus on their positive or negative feelings about themselves. If we're among the small percentage of women with naturally high self-esteem, we might think, *I feel good about myself and my abilities*. But if we're among the majority of women who struggle with low self-esteem, we may say to ourselves, *I hate who I am — I wish I could change my traits and personality*. In order to boost low self-esteem, women are often encouraged to love themselves and admire their qualities.

Self-worth, on the other hand, focuses less on feelings of self-love and more on the *value* we believe we have. As Christians, we should perceive our "worth," first, in the context of our relationship with God. We are made in His image, and by His loving us and choosing us, He grants us worth.

Sadly, many women — even committed Christian women — have too low a view of their worth. Our behavior, in turn, is guided by our view of ourselves — our self-image. Self-image is the internal portrait we each have that illustrates how we *really* feel about ourselves. If we were to paint with words an honest self-portrait, that would be our self-image. The shades and angles of our internal portrait reflect a lifetime of joys and pains, successes and failures.

The early and foundational brush strokes made by our parents and family provide the backdrop for our self-portrait. As women who are driven by and large to please others and achieve lofty goals, trauma, failure, abuse, and abandonment can distort and damage our self-image. Eventually, our distorted self-image changes our perception of our value as human beings and even our perceived value to God. Only the Lord who made us and gives us worth can erase the jagged lines and restore our portrait, granting us renewed confidence and contentment in how He has made us.

In order to develop an accurate understanding of ourselves, we must gauge our worth by God's assessment of us, not by comparing ourselves with others. A woman who has placed her faith in Jesus Christ can know she is God's adopted daughter.

Have you come to grips with your position in the family of God? It's essential! Through experiencing God's unconditional acceptance, you can know how highly He values you and that you have infinite worth.

My Story

A woman's self-worth and self-image, for better or for worse, are closely connected to her relationship with her earthly father. As her first introduction to her heavenly Father, a girl's earthly father prepares her heart to trust or distrust God. If a little girl has a loving, emotionally present father who affirms, encourages, and shares healthy physical affection with her, she will be much more likely to live with confidence, self-worth, and an accurate self-image. On the other hand, an absent or abusive father can damage a young girl, causing painful wounds that only God can heal.

Though we shouldn't play the blame game without taking responsibility for our lives and decisions, we also must face the dark areas of our past that have made us who we are today—trusting in God to bring wholeness and an accurate view of our worth in His eyes.

I know firsthand the challenge of trusting in God after living my whole life without a father. I grew up as an only child, raised by a wonderful, loving, sacrificial, single mother. But I have never met my biological father. Though my mother met all of my physical and material needs, she could never fill the daddy-shaped hole that God designed my father to fill. She was never meant to fill that empty space.

As a young girl and through my teenage years, I struggled with very low self-esteem resulting from low self-worth and a broken self-image. At my best moments, I found happiness and worth in good grades and friendships, but in the darkest times, I questioned why I was even alive, sure that my existence was a mistake. Though I knew there was a God, I doubted whether He knew that I existed. And worse, I doubted that God even cared for me.

Feelings of profound aloneness, anger, and depression haunted me throughout my adolescent years until college when I heard and understood the gospel. From that point—from the realization that I wasn't a mistake but loved by the Lord—God began removing the distortions in my self-image and rebuilding my trust in Him. Depression, anger, and loneliness didn't dissipate immediately, but the process of healing started. Though I still struggle with anger and depression, I no longer doubt God's love for me and His presence in my life.

What Is a Biblical Self-image?

Before God created the first atom, He had you and me in mind (Ephesians 1:4). And before our ancient parents fell in the garden, the Son of God planned to step into humanity in order to adopt us into His heavenly family (Revelation 13:8). And now, the Holy Spirit assures us of our competence by empowering us to live godly lives (Romans 8:15–16) and fulfill God's purposes (Philippians 1:6).

I didn't always believe these truths. If you struggle to believe that you have inherent worth, take heart! It is possible to realign our thoughts about ourselves so we can view ourselves the way God sees us. This takes place within the context of authentic relationships with God and with people. God has used my wonderful husband, who accepts me just the way I am, in my healing process. I also have a loving, caring father-in-law who would do absolutely anything to help me. Slowly, I am learning to trust God as my Father and to know that He is really *there*.

The key to my transformation has involved reading and *believing* Psalm 139. If you struggle with low self-worth and a distorted self-image, I challenge you to read this psalm — *every day* — and meditate on each truth it reveals.

Consider these amazing truths: God searches your heart, knows everything about you, and loves you. He fully understands your thoughts and feelings even before you do. The Lord not only knows the steps you take but He analyzes and pores over them. He intimately cares for you, your decisions, and the fears and worries you hide in your heart. God knows every loving and angry word before it crosses your lips, and His sovereign hand keeps you right where He wants you at each moment. In your highest joys and your deepest despair, He stays close. In the darkness, He gives you light. And there's more! Your Creator designed you perfectly for His purpose, and He will use every pain, every distortion in your self-image to bring His light and hope to others.

Because I'm a mistake in the world's eyes, the truth in Psalm 139:13–16 hits home in my heart. The fact that God skillfully knit me together in my mother's womb and planned all my days before my first breath gave me self-worth and completely reframed my self-image.

God created and designed every woman to have a unique combination of temperaments, interests, abilities, and physical characteristics that make us who we are, unlike any other individual on the face of the earth. After God made you, He threw out the mold and will never use it again. You are beautiful in His eyes!

What Now?

As we begin to reframe our self-image to match God's view of us, here are some activities that can help us.

First, we can log our thoughts in a journal. For example, a woman who accidentally drops a dish and breaks it may instinctively think, *I'm so clumsy. I can't do anything without breaking something*. Further, more damaging thoughts may come to mind: *I'm never going to be good at anything. I'm a failure.*

Second, we can observe patterns of negative thoughts and recurring extreme statements, all-or-nothing thinking, and hopeless words, such as *always* and *never*. Also, we should note what we do in response to our negative thought patterns.

Third, we must probe to the root of our negative thinking. What false beliefs underlie our self-condemning thoughts? Perhaps we believe that we must be perfect in order to be worthy of love. Perhaps we define our worth by comparing ourselves with others.

Fourth, we should open a Bible, find Scripture to counter each negative thought pattern in our journal, correct our false beliefs and negative thinking, and begin to paint our portrait from God's point of view. When our feelings condemn us, we must choose to believe the true picture God's Word paints of us *and of Him*.

Fifth, we can write an actual self-portrait, accurately assessing our strengths and weaknesses, our gifts and struggles. We can include our physical features, history, talents, spiritual gifts, accomplishments, character qualities, and so forth.

Finally, keeping in mind God's Word and His work of transformation in our lives, we should describe our potential self. God has designed us as His image-bearers and His daughters. He wants us to love Him and others and to use the gifts He has given us to serve in His kingdom. What would your life look like and how would you feel if you were fulfilling God's purpose for you? This description can give you hope and a vision of a fulfilled, confident life.

God never intended us to live fearfully under a heavy cloud of brokenness and inadequacy. Our identity in Christ, our spiritual position as a result of God's justifying, redeeming, and reconciling work through Christ, now forms our self-worth. As we walk the path of repainting our self-image to match our worth in God's eyes, let's reflect on God's blessings in Ephesians 1. He has given us every tool we need to live out His calling on our lives. He has chosen and adopted us, given us endless resources of grace, and His powerful Spirit strengthens us to not only embrace our story but to share it with others.

Digging into Psalm 139

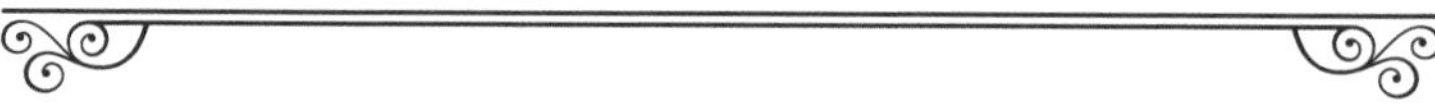

Psalm 139 opens the windows of heaven, giving us a glimpse into God's sovereignty, comprehensive knowledge, omnipresence, and intimate care and protection. Let's take a few moments to dig into this treasury of wisdom so that it might ground our self-worth in God's unconditional love.

Psalm 139:1–6 reveals God's omniscience — His complete knowledge of everything, from our secret thoughts and our every step, to our words before we speak them. Read and reflect on these six verses. Then, write down a few of your undisclosed hopes, dreams, and fears.

Next, write a prayer entrusting those hopes, dreams, and fears to God's sovereign plan for your life.

Psalm 139:7–12 displays God's omnipresence. No matter how alone we may feel on our most difficult days, God is always near. He is present and powerful in our lives as well as everywhere in the entire universe. With this in mind, read and reflect on Psalm 139:7–12. Record several times in your life when you recognized the evidence of God's presence in your life.

Next, write a prayer thanking God for His nearness and activity in your life.

Psalm 139:13–18 examines God's intimate weaving work of creation in the dark depth of a mother's womb, as He carefully knits together a human being. Read and reflect on this amazing passage and then write down some of the physical and personality characteristics you like least about yourself.

Remember that God lovingly arranged your DNA to make you unique! Write a prayer acknowledging that you are fearfully and wonderfully made, just the way you are.

Psalm 139:19–24 reminds us that God is just. He will hold accountable everyone who has made us feel inferior, ugly, or like a failure. The Lord will also examine our hearts and shine the light on any wrong ways of thinking and acting in our lives. Read and reflect on this passage. Then, write down any negative thought patterns—as well as the sources of those thought patterns—that affect the way you see yourself.

Next, write your own paraphrase of Psalm 139:23–24, and pray it every day for a week.

—Malia Rodriguez

How to Begin a Relationship with God

Life, a seemingly endless flurry of activity, sometimes leaves us wound up and dizzy. As we labor under a list of to-dos and unrealistic expectations, spiritual, emotional, and physical exhaustion will eventually take their toll. But God's Word provides the gentle reminder to *rest* — to sit at the feet of our Lord and receive *His* love and strength. Through the good news found in the Bible, the Lord breathes peace and contentment into our hearts. From Genesis to Revelation, God reveals four essential truths we all must accept and apply to receive the life-transforming help He promises. Let's look at these four truths in detail.

Our Spiritual Condition: Totally Depraved

The first truth is rather personal. One look in the mirror of Scripture, and our human condition becomes painfully clear:

> *"No one is righteous—*
> *not even one.*
> *No one is truly wise;*
> *no one is seeking God.*
> *All have turned away;*
> *all have become useless.*
> *No one does good,*
> *not a single one."* (Romans 3:10–12)

We are all sinners through and through — totally depraved. Now, that doesn't mean we've committed every atrocity known to humankind. We're not as *bad* as we can be, just as *bad off* as we can be. Sin colors all our thoughts, motives, words, and actions.

If you've been around a while, you likely already believe it. Look around. Everything around us bears the smudge marks of our sinful nature. Despite our best efforts to create a perfect world, crime statistics continue to soar, divorce rates keep climbing, and families keep crumbling.

Something has gone terribly wrong in our society and in ourselves—something deadly. Contrary to how the world would repackage it, "me-first" living doesn't equal rugged individuality and freedom; it equals death. As Paul said in his letter to the Romans, "The wages of sin is death" (Romans 6:23) — our spiritual and physical death that comes from God's righteous judgment of our sin, along with all of the emotional and practical effects of this separation that we experience on a daily basis. This brings us to the second marker: God's character.

God's Character: Infinitely Holy

How can God judge us for a sinful state we were born into? Our total depravity is only half the answer. The other half is God's infinite holiness.

The fact that we know things are not as they should be points us to a standard of goodness beyond ourselves. Our sense of injustice in life on this side of eternity implies a perfect standard of justice beyond our reality. That standard and source is God Himself. And God's standard of holiness contrasts starkly with our sinful condition.

Scripture says that "God is light, and there is no darkness in him at all" (1 John 1:5). God is absolutely holy — which creates a problem for us. If He is so pure, how can we who are so impure relate to Him?

Perhaps we could try being better people, try to tilt the balance in favor of our good deeds, or seek out methods for self-improvement. Throughout history, people have attempted to live up to God's standard by keeping the Ten Commandments or living by their own code of ethics. Unfortunately, no one can come close to satisfying the demands of God's law. Romans 3:20 says, "For no one can ever be made right with God by doing what the law commands. The law simply shows us how sinful we are."

Our Need: A Substitute

So here we are, sinners by nature and sinners by choice, trying to pull ourselves up by our own bootstraps to attain a relationship with our holy Creator. But every time we try, we fall flat on our faces. We can't live a good enough life to make up for our sin, because God's standard isn't "good enough"—it's *perfection*. And we can't make amends for the offense our sin has created without dying for it.

Who can get us out of this mess?

If someone could live perfectly, honoring God's law, and would bear sin's death penalty for us — in our place — then we would be saved from our predicament. But is there such a person? Thankfully, yes!

Meet your substitute — *Jesus Christ*. He is the One who took death's place for you!

> *God made Christ, who never sinned, to be the offering for our sin, so that we could be made right with God through Christ.* (2 Corinthians 5:21)

God's Provision: A Savior

God rescued us by sending His Son, Jesus, to die on the cross for our sins (1 John 4:9–10). Jesus was fully human and fully divine (John 1:1, 18), a truth that ensures His understanding of our weaknesses, His power to forgive, and His ability to bridge the gap between God and us (Romans 5:6–11). In short, we are "justified as a gift by His grace through the redemption which is in Christ Jesus" (Romans 3:24 NASB). Two words in this verse bear further explanation: *justified* and *redemption*.

Justification is God's act of mercy, in which He declares righteous the believing sinners while we are still in our sinning state. Justification doesn't mean that God *makes* us righteous, so that we never sin again, rather that He *declares* us righteous—much like a judge pardons a guilty criminal. Because Jesus took our sin upon Himself and suffered our judgment on the cross, God forgives our debt and proclaims us PARDONED.

Redemption is Christ's act of paying the complete price to release us from sin's bondage. God sent His Son to bear His wrath for all of our sins—past, present, and future (Romans 3:24–26; 2 Corinthians 5:21). In humble obedience, Christ willingly endured the shame of the cross for our sake (Mark 10:45; Romans 5:6–8; Philippians 2:8). Christ's death satisfied God's righteous demands. He no longer holds our sins against us, because His own Son paid the penalty for them. We are freed from the slave market of sin, never to be enslaved again!

Placing Your Faith in Christ

These four truths describe how God has provided a way to Himself through Jesus Christ. Because the price has been paid in full by God, we must respond to His free gift of eternal life in total faith and confidence in Him to save us. We must step forward into the relationship with God that He has prepared for us — not by doing good works or by being a good person, but by coming to Him just as we are and accepting His justification and redemption by faith.

> *God saved you by his grace when you believed. And you can't take credit for this; it is a gift from God. Salvation is not a reward for the good things we have done, so none of us can boast about it.* (Ephesians 2:8–9)

We accept God's gift of salvation simply by placing our faith in Christ alone for the forgiveness of our sins. Would you like to enter a relationship with your Creator by trusting in Christ as your Savior? If so, here's a simple prayer you can use to express your faith:

> *Dear God,*
>
> *I know that my sin has put a barrier between You and me. Thank You for sending Your Son, Jesus, to die in my place. I trust in Jesus alone to forgive my sins, and I accept His gift of eternal life. I ask Jesus to be my personal Savior and the Lord of my life. Thank You. In Jesus' name, amen.*

If you've prayed this prayer or one like it and you wish to find out more about knowing God and His plan for you in the Bible, contact us at Insight for Living Ministries. Our contact information is on the following pages.

We Are Here for You

If you desire to find out more about knowing God and His plan for you in the Bible, contact us. Insight for Living Ministries provides staff pastors who are available for free written correspondence or phone consultation. These seminary-trained and seasoned counselors have years of experience and are well-qualified guides for your spiritual journey.

Please feel welcome to contact your regional office by using the information below:

United States

Insight for Living Ministries
Biblical Counseling Department
Post Office Box 5000
Frisco, Texas 75034-0055
USA
469-535-8397 (Monday through Friday, 8:00 a.m.–5:00 p.m. central time)
www.insight.org/contactapastor

Canada

Insight for Living Canada
Biblical Counseling Department
PO Box 8 Stn A
Abbotsford BC V2T 6Z4
CANADA
1-800-663-7639
info@insightforliving.ca

Australia, New Zealand, and South Pacific

Insight for Living Australia
Pastoral Care
Post Office Box 443
Boronia, VIC 3155
AUSTRALIA
1300 467 444

United Kingdom and Europe

Insight for Living United Kingdom
Pastoral Care
PO Box 553
Dorking
RH4 9EU
UNITED KINGDOM
0800 787 9364
+44 1306 640156
pastoralcare@insightforliving.org.uk

Resources for Probing Further

Exquisitely Imperfect: Choosing Life Unfiltered was written to affirm the issues that we face as women every day, and as an encouragement to pause and reconnect with the Lord in an honest and meaningful way. We hope that this book strengthens a lifelong commitment to seek God through His Word. Along this journey, you might find yourself looking for other resources. We've listed several below. Of course, we cannot always endorse every assertion a writer outside of Insight for Living Ministries makes, so we encourage you to approach all other resources with wisdom and discernment.

Clark, Linda. *5 Leadership Essentials for Women: Developing Your Ability to Make Things Happen*. Birmingham, Ala.: New Hope, 2004.

Glahn, Sandra. Coffee Cup Bible Studies Series. Chattanooga: AMG, 2006–2013.

Hughes, Barbara. *Disciplines of a Godly Woman*. Wheaton, Ill.: Crossway, 2006.

Insight for Living. *Releasing Worry and Finding Worth as a Woman*. Plano, Tex.: IFL Publishing House, 2009.

Shirer, Priscilla. *A Jewel in His Crown: Rediscovering Your Value as a Woman of Excellence*. Chicago: Moody Publishers, 2004.

Spangler, Ann and Jean E. Syswerda. *Women of the Bible: A One-Year Devotional Study of Women in Scripture*. Grand Rapids: Zondervan, 2015.

Swindoll, Charles R. *Esther: A Woman of Strength and Dignity*. Great Lives Series. Nashville: Thomas Nelson, 2008.

Ordering Information

If you would like to order additional copies of *Exquisitely Imperfect: Choosing Life Unfiltered* or other Insight for Living Ministries resources, please contact the office that serves you.

United States

Insight for Living Ministries
Post Office Box 5000
Frisco, Texas 75034-0055
USA
1-800-772-8888
(Monday through Friday, 7:00 a.m.–7:00 p.m. central time)
www.insight.org
www.insightworld.org

Canada

Insight for Living Canada
PO Box 8 Stn A
Abbotsford BC V2T 6Z4
CANADA
1-800-663-7639
www.insightforliving.ca

Australia, New Zealand, and South Pacific

Insight for Living Australia
Post Office Box 443
Boronia, VIC 3155
AUSTRALIA
+61 3 9762 6613
www.ifl.org.au

United Kingdom and Europe

Insight for Living United Kingdom
PO Box 553
Dorking
RH4 9EU
UNITED KINGDOM
0800 787 9364
+44 1306 640156
www.insightforliving.org.uk

Other International Locations
International constituents may contact the U.S. office through our Web site (www.insightworld.org), mail queries, or by calling +1-469-535-8436.